15

Vilhelm Ekelund
THE SECOND LIGHT

Translated and with an Introduction by Lennart Bruce

With an Afterword by Eric O. Johannesson

NORTH POINT PRESS / SAN FRANCISCO / 1986

In my selection of the aphorisms I have taken into account a
desire once expressed by Vilhelm Ekelund to publish a new
edition that would combine *Plus Salis* and *Atticism–Humanism*. He thought the two would appropriately balance each
other. As always, though, this idea was mentioned as if in
passing: "There really exists no book of mine" (see Introduction, page xviii).

K. A. Svensson was a librarian, longtime friend, and practically a Boswell of Ekelund. He was the author of *Vilhelm
Ekelund, Moralisten—Kulturkritikern* (*Vilhelm Ekelund, the
Moralist—Culture Critic*), 1946, Fritzes, Sweden; and *Vilhelm
Ekelund i Samtal och Brev, 1922–1949* (*Vilhelm Ekelund, Conversations and Letters, 1922–1949*), 1958, Gleerups, Sweden.
(Svensson was awarded the distinction of honorary doctor at
the University of Lund, Sweden, for his work.) During my
last meeting with him shortly before his death, he expressed
his high esteem of *Elpidi* among Vilhelm Ekelund's work.

I have taken these remarks into account in order to pay
homage to both men.

I have also put certain emphasis on *The Second Light* and
Traces and Signs, which have meant a great deal to me personally. To make a smooth transition from Vilhelm Ekelund's
earlier work to his latter, I have also included aphorisms
from *Metron* and *Between Passions*.

Grateful acknowledgment is extended to Anne-Marie Eke-
lund-Hedlund, holder of copyright for the original Swedish
editions of Vilhelm Ekelund's writings, for permission to
publish these translations; to *Delos 2: A Journal on and of
Translation*, for excerpts from *Agenda* and *Nordic and Classic*,
copyright © 1968 by the National Translation Center, Austin,
Texas; to *The Prose Poem*, edited by Michael Benedikt, for excerpts from *Agenda* and *Nordic and Classic*, copyright © 1976
by Michael Benedikt; and to *Alcatraz #3*, for "The Flowers of
the Destitute," copyright © 1985 by Stephen Kessler and
Hollis deLancy for Alcatraz Editions; and to the Archives of
the Bonnier Publishing Co., Sweden, and the Ulf Eriksson
collection, Sweden, for photographs of Vilhelm Ekelund.

Contents

Introduction:
Medicina Mentis

I am but an eye looking into the blind and ghastly eye of meaninglessness. Why? Who am I? The howling loneliness around the human.

Those were the first words by Vilhelm Ekelund I ever read. They stood out then, as they do here at the top of the page, in a kind of bas-relief that headed an essay about Ekelund in a Swedish literary magazine. His name was unknown to me but his words moved me in a strange way. Somehow they appeared surrounded by the blackness of space.

Perhaps I was receptive at the time because of a devastating life experience. I had been an entrepreneur involved in outlandish projects with Sweden as a base. I had balanced on a knife's edge of financial adventure, where success lay on one side, disaster on the other. Soon I was "cast off," plunging into the abyss. I pulled everything with me in the fall, the company I inherited from my father, the computer enterprise I started in the mid-fifties, the African companies: public transport, cold storages, supermarkets.

When the crash hit me I was in West Africa, a bad spot in which to go broke. Recalling those days I still feel the ominous danger with which my wife and I were surrounded: the fecund heat, the tropical bush with its cancerous growth, the torrential rains, clouds seeming to rest on one's eyebrows, the sickness and the poverty, the lack of medical care, and the lawlessness. Still, there are occasions when a "lawless" community becomes more humane than a "society of law and order." When reaching such a community's deepest layers, there sometimes remains a latitude for benevolence in its original form, free of legal technicalities, a pure compassion under utterly harsh conditions, a necessary goodness that emanates from the depths of the human soul.

Thus the Africans were the ones to go out of their way to assist us and help us escape from the vicious attacks of our white financiers. At the end of a long period of exhaustion, I became ill with malaria— I probably neglected my quinine tablets—and started hallucinating. It was as though my whole life had risen in phantasms around me in a huge wave that would not break. I was terrified, but at the same time I could not help being fascinated by the visions. They revealed a new dimension of my psyche that I had been unaware of until my subconscious began feverishly exploring the different layers of fear.

Strangely, as I tried to keep the shapes of the grotesqueries in my memory, they seemed to lead me toward a beginning, a fresh and changed concept of the world: "You are never any higher than at the beginning—better to crawl than to swell" (Vilhelm Ekelund).[1]

In my readings of Ekelund I found to my amazement the sentence: "Don't forget those for whom a sudden terrible experience became the key to the richness of life and spiritual vision—don't forget them! The boundlessly happy inner expansion that takes place when the doors to the outer world of desires have to be closed—don't forget!

"And in addition to this (if one draws on the future) always to live! Thus being relieved of all anguish of vanity and pride."

This was a perfect expression of my state of mind and the resulting recoil of the shock in the direction of survival: "So much in this man's life seems as though it were addressed solely to myself. Contemplate the possibility that you yourself could become a letter written to a recipient waiting somewhere in the future" (V.E.).

I had been touched by Ekelund's hands, cool enough to carry their treasure to me, while I was suffering from the burns inflicted in the tropical heat of equatorial Africa: "Light. The light puts out all pain. Light is the coolest of all" (V.E.).

His enduring words made me think of the granite cobblestones brought from Sweden to cover streets in the outskirts of Buenos Aires that I walked as a young man, when I lived there as an exporter of fruit to Europe. They proved to be as hardy and as difficult to tread.

[1]To indicate future quotations of Vilhelm Ekelund I will use his initials V.E.

Despite the ease with which Ekelund moved among the masters of antiquity, as well as the great Europeans—Goethe, Nietzsche, Rousseau, and others—on a perfectly equal basis, he had not become a literary household word like Strindberg, which I thought odd; indeed, he was not even as well known as those he had influenced among the Scandinavian modernists, such as Pär Lagerkvist or Gunnar Ekelöf. When I asked Swedish writers about his influence on them, the reply invariably was astonishment at my asking such a self-evident question.

The reason, I believe, is that Ekelund is, to use a Swedish expression, a "portalfigur" in Scandinavian literature (literally translated, a "portal figure," someone through whom everyone must pass). In different ways he has influenced all subsequent Scandinavian literature, from the Finns in the East (for example, Rabbe Enckell, Gunnar Björling, Edith Södergran) to the Norwegians in the West (including Olof Hauge, one of the greatest living Norwegian poets) to the Danes in the South (Peter Seeberg, for example).

When I tried to pinpont the nature of his influence on Swedish writers, I was led from one source to the other. Authors mentioned in this connection included names like Karl Wennberg and Sven Delblanc, and when I posed the question to writers like Östen Sjöstrand and Tomas Tranströmer, they unhesitatingly acknowledged Ekelund's influence and proudly showed their collections of his works.

Among others, the following Swedish writers and scholars have written extensively on Ekelund:

ALGOT WERIN. *Vilhelm Ekelund 1880–1908.* Published 1960.

ALGOT WERIN. *Vilhelm Ekelund 1908–1925.* Published 1961 (both Glerups Förlag, Lund).

PIERRE NAERT. *Stilen i Vilhelm Ekelunds aforismer och essäer.* (The style in the aphorisms and essays of Vilhelm Ekelund). Published 1949, Glerups Förlag, Lund.

NILS GÖSTA VALDÉN. *Grekiska termer hos Vilhelm Ekelund.* (Greek terms of Vilhelm Ekelund). Published 1961, Glerups Förlag, Lund.

CARL-ERIK AF GEIJERSTAM. *Det personliga experimentet.* (The personal experiment). Published 1963, Bonniers Förlag, Stockholm.

SVEN LINDQVIST. *Dagbok och diktverk, en studie i Vilhelm Ekelund, Nordiskt och Klassiskt.* (Diary and writings, a study of Vilhelm

Ekelund, Nordic and Classic). Published 1966, Bonniers Förlag, Stockholm.

PER ERIK LJUNG. *Vilhelm Ekelund och den problematiska författarrollen.* (The problematic role of the author). Published 1980, Liber Förlag, Lund.

EVA LILJA NORDLIND. *Studier i fri svensk vers, den fria versen hos Vilhelm Ekelund och Edith Södergran.* (Studies in Swedish free verse, the free verse of Vilhelm Ekelund and Edith Södergran). Published 1983, Litteraturvetenskapliga Institutet, Gothenburg University.

EVA-BRITTA STÅHL. *Vilhelm Ekelunds estetiska mysticism.* (Vilhelm Ekelund's aesthetic mysticism). Published 1984, Litteraturvetenskapliga Institutionen, Uppsala University.

The reasons Ekelund is not better known lie in his total openness, his uncompromising honesty, at times approaching arrogance, and his choice of subjects. Only the great questions of humanity interested him, and then in the densest form possible, expressed through the means of the aphorism: "The aphorism: the pragmatic literary form par excellence.[1] Wanderer's thought—contrary to paid thought.

"In the encounter and the happening solutus omni foenore.[2] Here is demarcation (aphorismēnon[3]).

"The fullness of the moment and its definition 'Ein würdiger Einschnitt in Zeit und Ewigkeit' (A worthy nick in time and eternity)" (V.E.).

Finally, feeling the lack of appreciation, bordering on outright hostility, his uncompromising nature forced him into a more and more cryptic mode of expression: "The Philistine has soiled the world, ruined and falsified the language to such an extent that perhaps one had better not express oneself except by secret formulas, codes, in a sibylline way." Also: "No one causes as much irritation as the one who goes against the tide—and at the same time maintains his openness and clarity. It is not with satire one challenges the insipid spirit most profoundly!

"There is a way to prolong life and give it strength by making the

[1]Of preference.
[2]Free of all gain.
[3]That which is demarcated.

right enemies: drawing the right nourishment from antagonism. On the strength of making such a move you might also find something of the cunning and shrewdness at the service of a dominant desire for indifference and coolness—like a heavy downpour, an intellect's cold shower on your feelings. Thus it was made possible for the human genius to exist at all: to endure the high pressure under which he has to go on living" (V.E.).

Ekelund also wrote: "There is a saying 'to sow wind and harvest storm.' But here is a person who could tell a few things about sowing storm without harvesting even a single puff of wind." Yet he had a lifelong faith in his own genius. It survived his bohemian student days, his years of destitute exile that brought him close to death, his many literary debacles. He maintained his strength through a merciless dissection of his own mind, where the struggle between pride and humility went on throughout his life—between an urge for recognition and the contempt of it: "There is no better compass than— fleeing. As long as there is something in you that is disgusted with yourself: (that flees) you are on a steady course, you are not abandoned" (V.E.).

Vilhelm Ekelund was a man of research within the discipline of aesthetics. His investigation of the human soul was truly scientific. He used the only tools available, his own thoughts, with a logic and self-exposure unique in world literature: "All my thought lies in the element of art. For me there is no thought without art" (V.E.).

He had the courage to face "the lie of one's life," the compromise between his ideal and his reality, at least rejoicing at the luxury of having an ideal, keeping it holy. Herein lies the secret of the therapy that Vilhelm Ekelund administered to himself with the rigor of obsession, a therapy that becomes eminently useful to anyone whose experience has forced him to the depths where "the doors to the outer world of desires have had to be closed."

He was attacked throughout his life and after his death. As late as 1972 the Swedish literary critic Madeleine Gustafsson wrote that Ekelund creates a world "built on an untenable foundation, eliminating people from his vision of life . . . as long as large areas of reality are excluded from it or looked upon as nonexisting, harmony cannot emerge in its totality."

Thus Vilhelm Ekelund is pictured as an introvert whose writings are useless for the average person in today's world. That nothing could be further from the truth was demonstrated to me not only by my own life experience, but also by other people living under pressure of a crisis that may best be described as "reality" in its purest form—when one is forced into a situation that strips one of everything but life—"when one is forced to stop theorizing and become a realist by experience: . . . without the affliction called power of experience, you are nevertheless someone poor in spirit.

"How gross the calculating thinker, the 'scholarly philosopher . . .' with regard to experience and practical knowledge, what grossness there is in such a concept as a 'practitioner by reasoning'!" (V.E.).

The reading of Vilhelm Ekelund is a most soothing therapy, especially in a society as competitive as ours. His words work against the grain of the aggressiveness with which one is constantly bombarded, an environment that Vilhelm Ekelund refers to as the "world of wrath," a world where one is taught to be uncritical of oneself, thereby limiting the means of self-advancement:

"There is no disgrace—so singular, ever so individual, solely and exclusively involving you, and attached to you, that you don't share and own together with everyone in the deepest sense of communion. But to this community (which is freedom) the road may be shorter and easier for you than for others, precisely by force of its solitary nature of being yours. Yes, it is from there you may rise, exactly from where it will hit you with the needle-sharp burn of singularity, at that most painfully complicated personal situation of your own and its danger point.—In what you fear most lies the clearest directions for your security. Character cannot be changed; but it becomes a battlefield for powerful forces by means of your vision's love, and light erupts where suffocation threatened" (V.E.).

At their roots Vilhelm Ekelund's concepts (see "Key Concepts in the Writings of Vilhelm Ekelund," p. xxiii) are indistinguishably entwined with the languages of antiquity—the Greek of Pindar, Plutarch, Homer. His concept of antiquity was a vision, an ideal which he would rediscover in the Upanishads', Bhagavad-Gita, Lao-tse, Confucius—in the West, almost exclusively among the mystics. He saw immortal words fly through the centuries like "birds of the sea

—their slender daring bodies glowing in the air!" "Many a time it seemed to me as if I had reached a joy above reason through this language (the Greek)—and thus the courage to live—in a way no other language had given me . . . Like the clouds of June/ the light around their fringes/ shining through the crown/ of a battered oak" (V.E.).

The latter image could represent Vilhelm Ekelund himself—the battered oak drawing energy from the earth through its gnarled roots, and from above the light through the crown, a kind of photosynthesis of the soul. He envied the dignity of the oak tree, torn as he was between humility and pride, empathy and detachment. The keenness of his relentless scrutiny of himself and his environment made him one of our greatest satirists, covering the whole spectrum from the solemn to the burlesque: "The starving: The starving understand each other. Who understood the dark gaze in Nero's eye better than Kierkegaard."—"Solid unpopularity is the only road to great influence."—"To stop. He had stopped. But whoever stops has nothing going for him—and then he starts to stink. And you can be sure that we will be kept aware of this activity of his."—"Into the dog's sense of life enters, no doubt as an essential fact, the joy that God created so many trees and lampposts for him to lift his hind leg against. If the literary critic's psyche could be analyzed, one would surely find there a vital, analogous disposition: the happiness that God, among the mass of harmlessly acceptable authors, created also the 'curious' and original, unacceptable ones for the critic to rush up to and lift his leg against" (V.E.).

He had a hot temper and he feared his wrath: "Wrath is omnivorous, there is nothing it won't use as a source of irritation . . . But holy rage is something else" (V.E.).

All through his life he feared being devoured by his fury, which could bring him to the verge of insanity. For example, while walking at night, he could be brought to a state of uncontrollable rage by an encounter with a car that had not dimmed its lights. Once, he rushed out in front of a car on a highway in southern Sweden, shaking his fist, yelling: "Put out your lights!" The driver managed to stop: "What do you mean, put out my lights!"

On another occasion he got so mad at a dancing couple in a restaurant who did not fulfill his esthetic requirements that he threw an ashtray at them on the dance floor. This type of behavior was also related to his loathing for "respectability," his distrust of honors and recognition. He had a panacea for this—to create scandal:

Ekelund was never invited to be elected a member of the Swedish Academy of Letters (neither was Strindberg). One time a member arranged a dinner party in order to give Ekelund the opportunity to meet some of his more illustrious colleagues. Ekelund arrived but was not very talkative. He went straight to one of the bookcases in the room where the guests gathered, looked very carefully, chose a thin volume that he started to read while standing in a corner. When it was time to go to the table, he brought the book with him. He chose to sit down at the place of honor and went on reading. Nobody dared to interrupt him. Then, just as the soup was about to be served, Ekelund closed the book, raised his ocean-blue eyes from the white tablecloth, and said: "One shouldn't socialize!" He rose from the table, took his hat and coat and left.

Only the person who told this story originally, Tage Aurell, a Swedish writer known for his laconic style, knows whether it is true. But the incident bears the true Ekelund mark. His supersensitivity, coupled with his frequently asocial behavior, created endless complications in his life.

A fit of rage also had dire consequences for his life and development as a writer. Late in the evening of June 28, 1907, Ekelund left a restaurant on an island outside Gothenburg, Styrsö. He was in high spirits after a couple of drinks. There was a garden with a fountain outside, and to amuse a friend's dog he threw a stick into the water. He happened to step on some plants next to the fountain. A man, unknown to him, tried to intervene. There was an exchange of words, which developed into an altercation. The man was in civilian clothes and not until later did Ekelund learn that he had beaten up the district police superintendent.[1] But it was for attacking a police officer "in the line of duty" that he was sentenced to a month in prison. When the Supreme Court upheld the ruling of the lower court in September of 1908, he fled to Berlin. He considered the ruling unjust

[1] From the local newspaper at the time, under the heading: POLICE SUPERINTENDENT ASSAULTED: "Mr. E. in particular proved to be a specialist in the crudest possible language and dealt the policeman such a violent blow beneath his left ear, he still suffers from the injury which impaired his mastication for a considerable time."

and refused to comply. He now faced exile for many years until the period for prosecuting his crime had expired.

He intended to make a living writing articles and books to be published in Sweden. In those days Berlin seemed far away, and it is always easy to ignore someone kept at a safe distance. Expected fees did not materialize. He sank deeper and deeper into poverty: "'Poverty is an endlessly long night,' says some knowing man. No, he did not know the poor! It is a day, unfortunately: an endless, painful day with a sharp and piercing light that smarts in the eyes . . . The matter goes deep and has an awesome reality. Utter destitution is a type of hypochondria that borders on insanity . . ." (V.E.).

He reached the bottom as a destitute after he had to leave Berlin in August of 1912, for fear of being involved in a confrontation with the police in a case that really concerned a friend. He left for Hamburg, where he lived a vagrant life under a fictitious name. In October, however, he was arrested for murder. He describes the incident in a letter: "Yesterday morning I was confronted with a playmate of the murder victim, who had seen the murderer (I was very worried, as the description of the suspect almost perfectly fit my appearance). He was startled when he saw me, but declared only minutes later that I was not the one. In a way I felt safe: my landlady in Berlin could testify that on the day of the murder, July 12, I was somewhere else. But in jail and during the interrogation I was subjected to horrible things . . ."

Afraid of being deported and handed over to the Swedish authorities, he traveled from one place to another. Practically penniless, he wrote to a friend: "I don't know how this will end. I now possess forty cents. Hope to find somewhere to stay overnight on credit, but then I'm out. My heavy overcoat seems to create panic, everything I wear is in rags, shoes torn. This is hell. In Berlin one could hide inside one's 'hole,' but here! That I haven't shot myself yet is only due to the fact that I have nothing to shoot with."

He sold his suspenders (he had found a rope to tie around his waist) and his coat.

From Hamburg he wrote in August 1911: "The only thing preventing me from dying is that I lack the means to kill myself in a somewhat decent and not too messy manner . . . I'm afraid of collapsing in the street. I might be deported as a vagrant at any time, as I sleep out at night and now the police are watching me . . ."

Slowly, however, things began to improve. A selection of his poems was accepted for publication as well as his translations of Leopardi and Lassalle. He could breathe again—but not too well in a physical sense! His hardships had taken their toll and at the end of December of that year he became seriously ill. In mid-January he had a lung operation and his condition was critical. He barely survived.

During the dark days of his vagrant life, with its increasingly accentuated desperation, he used the Heraclitean/Nietzschean paradox, the negative as positive, for a defense: that misfortune is "the dark, productive growing ground of noble fortune" (V.E.).

This high-strung roller coaster ride of nerves and feelings collapsed with the closeness of death, when many things can happen: "Is there any will of thought without will to power? Yes, one of indescribable sweetness—when you are close to death. Is this in your best interest?" (V.E.). Vilhelm Ekelund answered this question not only with words but also with his life. The proximity of death became a stepping stone for him. It broadened his vision to an extent that approached a rebirth of perception. He saw "the Second Light."

The affliction and slow healing of his lungs made him rediscover his breathing and its soothing rhythm, which not only restored his physical health but also gave him spiritual calm and expansion. To him the most essential thing was always to be at the beginning—arrival was a kind of death. The urge for a "vita nuova" was among many other things he had in common with Dante. It made me remember a day in West Africa when after innumerable difficulties I managed to divert a transatlantic liner from its Buenos Aires to Stockholm course: the first light on that funnel in the far distance rising from under the curvature of the ocean, carrying my colors, entering my port for the first time ever. To me this symbol of new beginnings was reaffirmed and enforced by Vilhelm Ekelund.

"Collapse" indicates something sudden, perhaps what comes to underlie a slow and patient movement toward change, and always appears in a flash, a revelation, half-submerged in the subconscious.

Ekelund's writings from then on showed a displacement of his antiquity ideals from pre- to post-Socratic, in the sense that Aeschylus, Pindar, and Sophocles remain, while Heraclitus, like Nietzsche, is revalued. Nietzsche's earlier works are praised, whereas his later are criticized: "On the road to self-knowledge, strongest self-determination, there is no phenomenon in recent history of civilization that has been of greater value to me than Nietzsche. He drove me back to sources of soundness in my nature, and I became his most ardent and grateful antagonist. The music of human enlightenment exposed me to its radiation down to the roots of my being" (V.E.).

But this revaluation was not achieved overnight: "Evenness is the friend of salt—and permanence. Keen and sharp—one day's work after the other!" (V.E.). The tempo of his life changed from *presto* to *lento*: "To become accustomed to the incorrigibility of conscience; to be able to foresee the attacks. (Beware of the unexpected, the sudden.) Yes, so it has to be. And the hope of something useful—of healing words and discovery words—can thus be nourished (relative honesty . . .)" (V.E.).

Reading Vilhelm Ekelund has truly been for me a "medicina mentis." Whenever in despair at the slowness of development and its futility, learning about his life and his reactions has been of the greatest help—the threats, the exile, the times of poverty, the humiliations, even his reactions to what, for an instant, might have been interpreted as success—and above all the importance of not becoming attached to material trappings, to be "detached."

Vilhelm Ekelund's most original work, without precedent in literature, stems from the time when he began the more demanding adaptation of his world to the concepts of "metron/lowliness" (from the end of the 1920s until his death in 1949). His latter writings are his so-called cryptic works. He intentionally cloaked his aphoristic prose in an armor of hermeticism, although his inner aim was clarity: "It is a passion for clarity and distinctness that predestines an author's work to unpopularity" (V.E.).

Nevertheless, his earlier writings are among the most original and modern in Scandinavian literature. The totality of his work has a remarkable amplitude, diversity, and richness. It will survive, but not as part of any major current of the times. He was and remains a loner, but he dealt with the great questions that are part of the unique human situation. Thus he became an innovative gatherer and conveyor of information.

His thought and language had the strength to bridge the dualism of the human condition. At the same time that it created a distance, it brought him close to reality "in a nutshell" ("in nuce"). Although Vilhelm Ekelund always wrote about the precariousness of the human situation, he rarely alludes directly to the atrocities of his days, although they certainly abounded.

Vilhelm Ekelund aimed at the highest level of human communication. One of his titles, "Bow and Lyre" (used on two occasions, 1912 and 1932), points in the direction of a universal language; of vibration; tone, as though suspended in the void of its motion, its sound, there existed a harmony contained by its tension. Generally, his title has been divided into two symbols: the tension between the bow, an instrument of war, on one hand, and the lyre, a tool of art, on the other. But there is a string common to both, and there is the world of matter and the quiver of the atomic nucleus, where the borderline between wave and vibration dissolves.

All his life Ekelund believed in the value of his work. He knew that only with the passage of time would his art stand out: "I was naïve enough to believe that some young and bold person would one day come up to me, reaching out his hand in alliance. I won't live to see that day—but my work will" (V.E.). He knew that "fame" is a name for the rutting scene, where art is marketed.

Vilhelm Ekelund died at the age of sixty-nine, working incessantly, although very ill. During his lifetime he published eight collections of poetry and twenty-four books of aphoristic prose and essays. Eight volumes were published posthumously, including two volumes of his letters. The Vilhelm Ekelund Society in Sweden continues to publish works by and about him.

He wrote: "I look upon (my writings) this way—that I can hardly expect any understanding or impact of my work lifted out of the whole process of development . . . the enlightening and provoking in my writing lies more in the history of its movement and the manner in which it untangles (life struggle) than in any separate concentration of thoughts, any isolated motif carried through. There really exists no book of mine."

He used world literature as a mirror in his profoundly personal analysis of the works of such writers as Pindar, Plutarch, Homer, Shakespeare, Goethe, Schopenhauer, Nietzsche, Dostoevski, Poe, Emerson, and Whitman, among others, and among the Scandinavians—Strindberg, Swedenborg, Kierkegaard, Ibsen, Brandes. He used their works as a point of departure to debate the situation of the writer and artist in modern society. His emotional engagement, his intellect, and his use of language make his works as modern and fresh as any contemporary writer's. His complex writings penetrate the mainspring of the human spirit and capture an element of timelessness. As expressed by the brilliant Swedish author Gösta Oswald: "He became my universities."

He knew that "human society has a memory of its own, far more durable and more varied than any individual belonging to it" (Norbert Wiener). When information is entered into these greater memory banks and referred to often enough, "refreshed," its life is prolonged. If little or no reference is made, the entry fades, the information is "forgotten." Thus the great essay is written without a pen in a gigantic scheme of preservation/elimination. In this manner Heraclitus, Pindar, Plutarch, and Homer, Ekelund's mentors, live on.

The loner Vilhelm Ekelund called what he tasted "the wine of dream, blood of word," and he let it tirelessly flow out into the void, bits of information from language's lips of the biosphere. Among them are these notes collected posthumously by Per Erik Ljung:

Dreams That Oblige

—but the adventure of a purified fighting spirit
could as a fairy tale in a way be made into the
blood of our blood: it is a question of
dreaming forcefully.
"The cult of dreams," that would be a themata
of mine. It could be advanced further.

To dream forcefully—
would that be our deliverance? The strong dreamers—
would they eventually prove to be the species,
the true bearers of—a feat of humanity?

All human digging, drilling, treasure hunting is
—in a true sense—a digging for freedom. Every major
quest is a search for the conditions of freedom.
This is the great anthropology.

and how the whole life of such a person may look like
that of the confused bird insisting on passing through
the closed window!—No matter how many doors and windows
are left open next to it, it persists in flying
toward the semblance of freedom.

The problem can be expressed in the simplest
possible way: the achieving of Lightness.
And it can be solved!

If we loved lightness, we would all be
heroes. But what we call "life" (and what is really its
opposite) outwits us.

A shade of daylight in your house, your body, your soul—
the particular one which is yours: your life depends
upon its upkeep. This economy (in the literal sense
of the word!) is the best moral.

The explanation of the world's misfortune
lies in the bootlicker mentality, the slavishness.

The secret passion called future:
which in every great life
is the counterbalance of other passions—counterbalance,
secret anchorage!

The grip and its firmness—only around the most
untenable. Therefore one's strength is:
faithfulness to the dream, so it was for all—
willed dreamers.

Productive method
—Those who understood to let their thoughts
lie in the sun, to them (Lichtenberg was one!)
I have to count myself. This method, this instinct
was my "diligence."

Abbreviations—for the purpose
of self-suggestion, definitely not because of
impatience, disorderliness.

The idyl: "Ice and honey."

The dream of a poetry, of the work of an author
totally spontaneous, the pure projection of music
in the highest sense, mystic, free revelation of law:
the Orphic dream, the hint of the possibility of
playing fair. Quietism's will to power,
its war.

Inexhaustible to experience, inexhaustible
to hope: as an author should be.

Lennart Bruce
February, 1985

Using the Guide to Key Concepts (p. xxiii) and the Index (p. 184)
To locate passages in this selection of Vilhelm Ekelund's writings, please refer to the marginal notations in the text, which list book, page number, and
aphorism number of the original Swedish editions. For book title abbreviations, please see the list on p. 183.

Key Concepts in the Writings of Vilhelm Ekelund

Everyone should enter Vilhelm Ekelund's world of concepts on his own and be aware of a difficult, if intriguing task. For this reason I have interpreted some of his key concepts (based upon his own sentences) for the reader's use or rejection. For the same purpose at the end of the concept sections, I have listed some of the aphorisms that relate to them. Their complexity opens them up to a wide range of interpretation, and even if my comments don't coincide with the reader's trend of thought, they may serve as suggestions for different directions of thinking.

Ekelund writes: "Enlightenment is only experienced by the few who possess a rare clarity of spirit. And exactly this clarity is the most obscure of all obscurity for the majority." For him the multifaceted significance of things had a greater fascination than the unambiguous. His concepts are building blocks linked together by an inner logic.

APHORISMENON: Demarcation, separateness; hence its special meaning, aphorism. "The writer of aphorisms is a 'literate' people's poet. An aphorism is as durable as is only pure didactic poetry . . . People of solitude always love the aphorism. It gives distraction to the hypochondriac, it gives an air of composure and calm to the nervous, it gives the illusion of productivity to the thinker and the poet in times of barrenness and nonproductivity. But it may also—and that is the true aphorism—be developed into a minute, concentrated, and stylish piece of art; through the highest degree of economy and energy it may measure up to the harmonious tension of perfect verse . . . If, of all literary forms, the aphorism is the one most profoundly limited, this should also indicate that—in order to have any meaning—it is also the most profoundly limiting form and as such precisely—unlimited—'a worthy nick in time and eternity'" (V.E.).

E102#7; AH80#51; PS115#4, #5; PS122#17; PS123#18.

METRON, METRICS: (Right, full) measure; bordering on the divine—the caress of the limitless borderline defining beauty; boundary of utter energy, the light it emits; vibration, tone; style; Tao. "Devoutness to feeling gives measure; irreverence, lack of piety is always without direction, lacking demarcation."—"*Metron* is the regal prayer, the mighty call of self-warning from someone who senses the possibility of perfection, the appeal to the forces of limitation in his soul . . ." (V.E.).

M25#19; M78#114; M101#128; BP127#223; AH46#90; PS66#10; PS90#4; PS122#17; AM62.

JOURNEY: From metron follows a readiness for journey, for continuation. "He whose heart has been seized by music understands that human spirit cannot die, as law cannot die. The clear conscience is an *entelechia*: ever continuing, ever expanding—journey" (V.E.).

AG47#5; BP177#330; BP179#335; BP186#347; TS27#12; SL208 #301; E17#26; AH30#58; AH37#71; AH117#27; AH123#41; AH125#45; AH141#2; AH142#4; PS150#2.

ENTELECHIA: Continuation; tenor—"The way of beauty is entelechia: the thought of continuation . . . Life is full of sparks, splashes of sun: accumulate to become sun—before the dark overwhelms you . . ." (V.E.); right to life; spiritual perpetuum mobile; soul.

AG92#28; VS127; PS66#10; NW40#121; SL228#342.

ATTICISM–HUMANISM: The essence of pure human metron. Through quietism, poverty, distance, unattachment toward the formula metron–elpis–*entelechia*; associated with Oriental thought, seeing and breathing; theme which makes metron into journey, Tao, a continuum, ocean without shores.

BL89#66; AH31#61; AH32#63; PS69#15; PS90#3; PS108#25.

PLAY: Play, aimlessness and music. "Play, the artistic play without intended gain—home of real freedom of movement." ". . . to play with them (sentiments)—but playing with them as though in earnest. It is this beautiful game that is also called—art . . ." (V.E.). BP120#213; BP155#285; BP156#286; BP170#318; E105#13; PS110 #30.

MUSIC: As opposed to the general interpretation, it refers to art in the widest sense as represented by the Greek Muses. Ekelund's art is no *ars poetica* but the art of life.
BP143#256; BP214#400; BP216#403; TS78#7; SL22#39; AH92#8; AH93#11; AH103#28; AH122#39; AH134#63; PS79#12; PS92#8; PS110#30; PS122#17; SH57#33.

CHARIS: Grace—"The golden fringe around an unobstructed day, life overflowing through it (and the 'sting' that leads there)"— "snow and roses"—"a scent of the secret of secrets" (V.E.).
M25#19; M101#128; SL151#168; E105#13; AH99#22; PS124#20; PS124#21.

BOUNDARY: Defining center, *in nuce*, and thus boundless, divine. "I wrote: on the boundaries is the finest light. I could also have written: on the boundary is the light. Eye and boundary . . . the meeting and the boundary . . . the god of its light . . . blood of my will's holiest heritage to culture" (V.E.).
TS65#49; E199#21; PS67#11.

DISTANCE: *Esse*, to be (at home) requires distance from "away."
TS15; AH21#38; AH22#41; AH23#44; AH24#46; AH40#77; AH99 #23; AH142#4.

SALT: Spice, taste in the widest sense—(associated with the Greek *kairos*: right in time, and with the Latin *otium*: free time)—"The Roman '*sal*' has an element of joy, an intimacy, captured by no translation" (V.E.). "*Plus salis quam sumptus*: more taste than luxury" (Cornelius Nepus).
NC78#147; E56#41; E98#36; E98#37; AH7#8; AH30#58; AH112 #15; AH113#16; AH132#59; AH170#2; SH38#69.

EGOISM: To conquer oneself by self-subjugation is for Ekelund simply a higher form of egotism.
AG49#10; M55#63; E17#26; PS123#19.

ENKRATEIA: Composure, self-control, rule. The restraint of content in the sense of to contain something fully, as the instant; a cool fire; joy in abeyance, leading to unintentionality, spontaneity.

BP50#77; BP111#193; BP136#244; BP141#254; TS76#5; E5#1;
E5#3; AH28#56; AH119#32; AH124#42; PS103#17; PS103#19;
PS123#19.

AUTOMATON: Spontaneity; voluntary action.—"In the soul's land
of possibilities there seems to be a territory where the intention is
the voluntary and the voluntary the intention" (V.E.).

M33#34; BP183#341; BP195#364; CA195#228; PS144#5.

APORIA: Hardship, in straits. According to Ekelund, freedom, liberation may be harmed by being successful but protected by *aporia*, adversity: "Whoever holds in contempt all other prices of victory but hope, never feels despair" (V.E.).

NC52#73; BP62#101; BP90#153; BP214#400; BP219#410; BP225
#422; TS5; TS17; E15#23; E21#31; AH47#93; AH129#55; PS103
#16; NW6#4; NW109#327.

PENIA—POVERTY—HUNGER: Of a platonic, mystic nature giving birth to love—Eros of true beauty, unattachment.

OTOS232; WE205; BP90#153; TS15#11; SL231#2; E17#26; E18#27;
AH49#97; AH93#10; AH103#29; AH132#59; PS86#1; PS101#14;
PS120#14.

DETACHMENT—DISINTEREST: Free of all gain. "See and love—
without envy—all richness, fullness, happiness—but above all—
have *ownership* and *disinterestedness*: the holy absurdity, home of
art and thought" (V.E.).

BP166#308; E18#27; AH47#93; AH145#10; PS5#25; PS15#26;
PS87#4; PS92#8; PS100#13.

UNATTACHMENT: "*Solutus omni foenore* (free from all usury)"—
Horace.

AG49#10; E13#17; AH117#27; AH143#5; AH145#10; PS100#12;
PS100#13.

ASKESIS: Practice, training.

E32#50; AH23#44; PS167#15.

SECURITY: To feel values and dignity threatened every moment—
then there is life, *security*. Then there is calm.

TS57#35; TS61#42; BL150#76; E100#4; PS15#25; PS179#34;
ISCL118#44; SH185#17.

ELPIDI: (make sacrifice) to hope, the hope of beginning's and innovation's joy; to the possibility of human truthfulness—of not
suffocating in one's own wretchedness. "Perhaps this is what the

life struggle (warfare) shall ultimately be about: the ability to sustain a searching, a scrutinizing eye, clear and full of hope.—My whole composition—for life's work and the day: my right to make sacrifice to hope, to serve and stand fast in order to be able to make sacrifice to hope" (V.E.).

E22#32; E105#13; AH47#93.

DEINOTES: A powerful force, "something 'demonic,' secretly at work—perhaps something akin to the mesmeric influence exercised by certain great conquerers in the field."—". . .corresponding to the 'demonic,' according to Goethe, in the character of, for example, Byron" (V.E.).

BP129#228; E103#9; AH10#18.

INDUCEMENT: "He who is constantly exposed to crudeness and crushing weight gains the splendid *inducement* to always think of that which is light, fleeting" (V.E.).

TS88#9; AH23#44; AH44#87; AH95#15; PS115#5; PS150#2; NW5#1; NW33#99.

ANANKE: Compulsion, necessity, inducement—to freedom and voluntariness. "The *ananke* of art: the enigmatic point—of freedom and guard—where freedom and compulsion prove to be one" (V.E.).

VS44; NC29#13; E100#4; E105#13; E130#1; SH75#11; SH98#13; SH185#17.

(LINE OF) DIRECTION: Vein, the vein of one's hope, one's belief, to maintain its line of direction; course.

VS112#7; BP37#51; BP131#232; TS29#3; E13#18; E103#8; AH123#41; PS103#17; PS118#12; PS177#30.

AUTHADEIA: Nonconformity; against the current; of one's own mind.

AG81#27; IL289; BP71#120; E108#17; AH22#42; AH32#63; AH33 #64; AH38#74; AH99#23; AH113#19; PS157#2; PS162#9; PS163 #10; PS165#12; PS167#15; PS171#19; PS179#34.

EUPHEMIA: Eloquence—to speak good, fortunate words, also in the sense of withholding the bad ones; conciliation of contrasts: glacier and summer, ice and honey, idyl.

E102#7; E131#3; E131#4.

MYSTICISM: "Where the dream—founded on metron, on mysticism—was dreamt purely and profoundly, there all confessions merged."—"What is it that we love in clarity? Is it not its mysticism?"—"The real poet is a mystic. He knows the human, not the humans . . . The historic connection between concepts follows via mysticism" (V.E.).

VS15#4; VS42/43; MW190; BP127#223; BP261#500; E131#3; AH93#10; AH96#17; AH145#10; PS67#11; PS79#12; PS86#1; PS101#14.

FORM: Also the interplay between art and the art of living.

BP48#72; SL95#36; E101#5.

PHILOLOGY: Literally "love of words;" for Ekelund: love of words that are lived. "The power of deep resonance built upon the close correspondence between the foundations of thought and living" (V.E.).

TS97#5; TS98#8; CA164#168; AH24#46; AH28#56; AH145#10.

MISOLOGY: Literally "hatred of words;" i.e., words that are not lived, experienced.

E9#11; PS92#9; PS122#17.

THE WANDERER'S THOUGHTS: Literally, thoughts arrived at while wandering in nature as opposed to thoughts contrived while sitting at a desk; also used in a broad sense: "To live one's thoughts by living up to them: where is there a lovelier hopefulness to be found than in the misology that bases itself on the obligation to live the motifs of one's thoughts—live them, to obtain the right to own them, right to make them reality" (V.E.).

AH24#46; PS99#10; PS103#16; PS115#4; PS146#8; SH98#13.

EGERIA—NUMA: Refers to the meetings between Egeria and Numa, Roman mythological lovers.—The resplendent boundary where the human and the divine meet; escape to nature, literally and spiritually.

E199#21; PS57#39; PS87#3; PS99#10; PS120#14.

TRACES AND SIGNS: "What do we call reality, values that we live by, security?—traces and signs of a divine life that was lost to the soul?" (V.E.).

MW190; TS57#34.

THEMATA—CHREMATA: "My themes are my property" (Greek). These words were inscribed on Vilhelm Ekelund's gravestone according to his wishes: "the breakthrough of this principle became the source that gave me continuous thought and the possibility of a life as an author" (V.E.).

TS74#7; AH121#37.

ELIKRINES: Pure, genuine, unadulterated. "A sense of language, an Eros relationship to language of the kind I preconceived, as also did Jung-Stilling—and followed in holy bliss and worship, it could be a way to expand, to find security and lodestar for a bright journey" (V.E.).

AG48#7; NC55#82; VS75#18; VS159#60; VS169#86; E131#3; AH44 #87; PS113#34.

EROS: Also in a wider sense, *Eros uranios* (Plato), a love of truth as opposed to pretense and lie. "A frame of mind and heart as preconceived by the Eros of my will . . ." (V.E.).

M35#36; BP90#153; TS90#1; TS93#4; SL151#168.

CONCORDIA ANIMI: Unanimity of the soul; close harmony between one's life and one's thought.

BP47#69; TS98#8; E16#24.

NEWNESS: The great art of youthfulness, to perceive and sustain the first lights, *Vita Nuova* (Dante), always to be at a beginning. Newness, innovation as opposed to "news," and its distractions: plan—not plans. "Only he who has *direction* is capable of newness. Others have—variations, news.—No news could be expected from me; I was too deeply immersed in newness" (V.E.).

AG41#17; VS142#18; BP131#231; BP131#232; BP131#233; BP133 #236; BP136#242; BP136#244; BP137#245; FTNF306; E22#32; E91#17; E96#30; E97#32; E98#38; CA7#1; AH93#12; AH117#27; AH129#55; AH132#59; AH133#62; AH141#2; AH168#33; AH169 #34; PS81#1; PS150#2; PS152#6; NW13#34; NW17#47; NW21 #58; NW22#59; NW40#121; ISCL118#44.

SCHOOL: Used by Ekelund in its original meaning, from Greek leisure, time for discussion, philosophy (Latin *otium*); and to always feel beginning, innovation, youth, set in the powerful light of spring.

PB175#326; AH49#97; AH168#33; PS152#6; PS152#7.

PRO DOMO (from Cicero): To be at home, in a consistent edifice built from spirit, life and day, to be able to live there. "*Content chez soi*" (Voltaire).

M64#87; TS26#10; TS54#27; E99#2; E100#3; AH10#18; AH40#77; AH93#12; AH124#42; AH125#44; PS123#19; PS152#7.

ASCLEPIADIC: Healing.

AG58#2; AG82#29; VS93; TS5; TS27#12; SL22#39; E141#11; AH49#96; AH51#100; AH94#13; PS69#15; PS118#12; NW6#4; SH57#33.

HELICHRYSUS: An immortelle, a flower of contrasts; the sun embodied in nature's growth and as such outstanding against its surroundings.

PS57#39; PS122#17.

CLIMATE: "How did I become a hunter for treasure? When I saw a climate (a land) in my nature, in the traditions of my blood which was my heritage. Then I began to realize that the strife of my whole existence was this: to prove my right to inherit . . . My climate is my whole plan of living and enlightenment. Climate is that which is alive, not the empirical. Climate: where I am a mine. What is a mine? Where one's property is" (V.E.).

TS88#9; TS89#10; TS89#11; E5#1; E18#27; CA74#11; AH7#8; AH94#13; AH94#14; PS100#13.

MINE (See *climate*): "The far-reaching, the clear and to-the-point always came out of the depth of a mine. The true *hekaergos* (far-shooting) Iliadian-Apollonian was always someone with the quality of a *mine* . . ." (V.E.).

BP262#501; AH46#89; AM61.

LOWLINESS, LOWNESS, EVENNESS: Modesty, humility; the widest perspective from the lowest point. "Without lowness—no ascending" (V.E.).

MW186; BP156#228; TS27#12; TS76#5; TS78#7; SL29#57; E7#7; E17#26; E28#44; E97#32; E108#17; CA7#1; AH49#97; AH93#10; AH99#22; AH113#19; AH116#25; AH124#42; PS120#14; SH38 #69; SH185#17.

BATHOS—PATHOS—ETHOS: Depth—height (*altitudo*). "Where do I want my pathos? Where my bathos is: my fertile lowliness and my plane, the richness of my humility . . ." (V.E.).

BP119#211; TS27#12; SL224#334; E130#1; AH113#19.

FOUNDATION—PROBABLE FOUNDATION: Ekelund uses the concept for ground, soil, root and the home of roots, source of nourishment (closely related to the concepts of mine, lowliness, climate). The probable foundation is one of Ekelund's more "opaque" crypticisms. The Ekelund scholar Pierre Naert indicates that V.E. uses the term "probable" with a strong tilt toward the original Latin meaning of something tested, proved, and found to be firm, solid, sound. Into the interpretation enters the suspicion that V.E. with his affinity for paradoxes hints at the living rock of mysticism, the one mountain not founded on a guess. "The attempt at truth, the experiment, begins only when one rises above *the probable foundation*. The bliss of height to look down upon a disaster one has escaped; to play with it—in order to feel joy" (V.E.). CA111#13; AH10#18; AH121#37; PS12#17.

EYE: "The care of the eye is true effacement; care of the eye by rhythm, time—the art of breathing—eye. Untimeliness: blindness in a deluge of fire."—"To *see* the human is the aim and meaning of all research and studies" (V.E.).
AG48#8; AG72#6; VS75; BP115#201; BP136#242; BP176#327; BP176#328; TS6; TS87#8; TS88#9; SL209#302; E97#32; AH8#10; AH43#85; AH79#50; AH96#16; AH99#22; AH141#2; PS101#14; PS122#17; AM62; SH26#35.

SUN: "An even accumulation of divine sunshine, slow and blissful, no artist's fever with repercussions of tumbling into darkness . . . My worship of the sun begins in the autumn, culminates in February" (V.E.).
AG92#28; M27#22; M28#23; BP166#308; BP169#316; TS66#51; AH132#59; NW40#121; SH176#33.

CYNICISM: Refers to the Greek *kynikos* and the ancient philosophers who stressed virtue and independence from worldly pleasures, and used by Ekelund in its original sense.
E123#2; AH94#13; AH94#14; AH95#15; AH119#32; AH134#63.

NIL ADMIRARI: To be astonished at nothing, to truly admire; the way great art sees.
OTOS238; BP186#347; BP216#404.

WAR, WARFARE: Used by Ekelund in the spiritual sense. "If the serene and pure reality of a warrior nature once became clear and alive in the minds and hearts of men, wouldn't war then, what we now call war, be utterly despicable?" (V.E.).
BP206#384; TS74#8; E28#44; E98#37; AH9#12; PS10#14; PS99#10; PS103#16.

ERIS: Contest. "Whoever made true struggle his bliss, he spreads the shine of gratefulness' sun over that which is darkest and most offensive in him. Tradition, that is, reciprocation—only reached by *contest*. One must live in a state of war, fighting even the dead."

Also: *"Hors concours"* (beyond competition) . . . "to the spirit of both a child and a giant the Greeks gave a name seldom understood—*Eris* . . . To have chosen—lowness! It is this fight and struggle—not the strife for position and power, one must love—as the most precious in life" (V.E.).

BP204#381; E32#50; AH7#7; AH10#18; AH99#22; AH118#31; PS72#1; PS177#30; PS179#34.

The Life of
Vilhelm Ekelund

The following selection of Vilhelm Ekelund's works emphasizes the later stage of his writing, the stage of an inner drama illuminating the themes he pursued with his feelings and thoughts (*Themata-Chremata*), which began at the time of his illness and crisis in 1913. Here I will give some chronological data, notes, and correspondence in order to illuminate Ekelund's earlier development.

Ekelund was born in Rönneholm, Stehag, in southern Sweden, October 14, 1880, the younger of two sons. His parents were Johannes and Johanna Ekelund. Johannes was a blacksmith, open and easygoing; Johanna was reserved and contemplative, and she encouraged Vilhelm's artistic inclinations.

In school Ekelund was a good student, but dependent on his teacher. When he lost interest in a subject, his mark would plummet from A to F.

His recollections from childhood and youth are bright and happy. He writes on the subject of Maxim Gorki: "Many times I have thought of writing a book about my childhood, but certainly of another kind than Gorki's. Why did I not carry through my intentions? I believe it is because my childhood was a happy one. A parallel is hard to establish. If my childhood had been as dark and desperate as Gorki's, I would probably have written that book long ago—I am afraid to plunge into this sea of sunlight, I feel unworthiness before these sacred years."

In 1894 the family moved to Lund, an academic center in southern Sweden. The parents wanted to provide better education for their sons.

Ekelund only held one salaried position in his life, in the summer of 1896, tutoring the son of a family in the neighborhood of Lund.

Ekelund was an ardent observer of nature. The landscape of his youth would stay with him throughout his life.

In 1900 he made his literary debut with a collection of poems titled *Vårbris* (*Spring Breeze*), followed by *Syner* (*Visions*) 1901, *Melodier i Skymning* (*Twilight Melodies*) 1902, *In Candidum* 1905, *Havets Stjärna* (*Star of the Ocean*) 1906, *Dithyramber i Aftonglans* (*Dithyrambs in the Glow of Evening*) 1906, and *Grekisk Bukett* (*Greek Bouquet*) 1906.

His books were well received. The leading critic of the time, Oscar Levertin, wrote: "Ekelund expresses in his poetry a mystical exultation that merges with nature in a peaceful, serene sacrament." Another critic added: "Twenty-three years old and Sweden's foremost poet."

In Ekelund's poems there is a suggestion of nature alluding to a corresponding inner landscape. He describes one of his wanderings in early spring:

> *It was here then, the forest at its best;*
> *washed clean and tidy*
> *tender grass—and the ground shone dark*

and later in the poem:

> *Something gruesome happened here.*
> *The firs lie strewn here and there*
> *they stumbled over one another—*
> *and the red wood split, bloody against the snow;*
> *screams and howls still linger in the air*
> *curses and coarse voices.*
> *What happened to you, anemones?*

It is no coincidence that an early short story has the title *"Oroligt Blod"* ("Turbulent Blood"). The predominant force counteracting the inner turbulence is the urge for beauty, in his poems a release, an act of love.

At the time he was mainly influenced by the German poets Platen and Hölderlin and the eighteenth-century Swedish poet Stagnelius.

His affinity for Platen was particularly strong. These lines made a lasting impression upon him:

> *Warm und hell dämmert in Rom die Winternacht:*
> *Knabe, komm! wandle mit mir, und Arm in Arm*
> *Schmiege die bräunliche Wang' an deines*
> *Busenfreunds blondes Haupt!*

(Dusk falls in Rome's winter evening / warm and full of light / Boy, come wander with me arm-in-arm / lean your tanned cheek on the blond head / of your bosom friend.)

Platen's secret, which Thomas Mann calls: "die lebensentscheidende Tatsache seiner exklusiv homoerotischen Anlage" ("His exclusive homophile inclinations, and its vital importance to his life"), had dawned upon Ekelund.

He shared the feelings of Platen and this inclination would also be of decisive importance in his life. He wrote to Amelie Bjärre (his confidant at the time, and whom he calls *Regina meae tristitieae* [Queen of my sorrow]): "When I discovered Platen I was nineteen years old and hardly understood a thing. Only *one* poem made an impression upon me. It was the one about the boy, "Winternacht in Rome" ["Winter Evening in Rome"]. The book remained on my shelf unopened until I was twenty-one years old. Then I understood. I then wrote a poem for him. I have never told anybody whom I referred to; it was my dream to once meet—it should by no means be a blond girl but a blond boy—who understood what I understood. Then, for the first time, I would be able to write out for him the name I had in mind. However, this never came about. What I here confide to you is really of no great importance because you will soon realize its meaning, the song in me."

Platen would follow Ekelund throughout his life. Their common inclination would also lead them both toward antiquity. In his essay on August von Platen Thomas Mann points to the art-psyche relationship with Plato's Eros. Ekelund writes:

> *Eros, Eros!*
> *What song*
> *delirious and barbaric*
> *you placed upon my mouth!*
> *and yet:*

does not a temple shine
within my soul
bright, serene
as the shine of dawn in spring"

He would praise Mann's *Der Tot in Venedig* (*Death in Venice*). He had traveled there himself and wandered the same streets that Mann's Gustav von Aschenbach did barely ten years later. Mann's character is based on Platen, and it was Platen who made Ekelund travel to Venice where he stayed for three months until he went broke.

Nevertheless, as is shown by his intimate letters to Amelie Bjärre, it was within the realm of his feelings to get emotionally involved with a woman as well as with a man. On the nature of this love he writes to her in 1906: "My wound is hardly of an erotic nature. Because I don't believe in this—for me! I never had that experience so deliriously praised—never in the common sense, but on the other hand, very strongly in a human mystic sense . . . but the sentimental eroticism, that modern invention, which antiquity did not even know existed. No! And it perishes on mere touch."

However, later, in 1913, Ekelund married the Danish nurse, Anne Margrethe Hou, who cared for him during his illness. The following year, their daughter Anne-Marie was born.

Hölderlin's attraction for Ekelund was of a different, although related kind. He wrote: "A true lyric poet may be a profound atheist in his daily thoughts—the innermost in his poetry remains in the sign of Buddha and Christ . . . Man's spirit shall always be forced to bring into focus the mystery of suffering, will never cease to search for the possibility of the great disharmony's mystic appeasement."

In trying to come to grips with the reason for Hölderlin's mental breakdown, Ekelund makes a surprising comparison with Whitman. He found in him a trait of coarseness characteristic for antiquity; a tough skin, a wintery virtue of deep human value which Hölderlin lacked in spite of his classic ideals: perhaps he was too weak, too good?

In *Concordia Animi* Ekelund points to Hölderlin's words: "I was crushed by my heroes." Ekelund himself used these words in one of his letters to Amelie Bjärre: ". . . Aeschylus, Pindar, Sophocles—are all I read. My love for Nietzsche brought me to those, his most intimate sources—and to the pre-Socratic philosophers. I was led on in the same direction by Hölderlin, Nietzsche's favorite poet; then by Platen. There you have my heroes. I fear that some day I will exclaim with Hölderlin, when he went to pieces: 'I was crushed by my heroes!' . . . Life is not easy to accept and that may be what makes the poet—in a positive sense: the ability to say yes, to embrace life, make peace."

With Hölderlin in mind Ekelund wrote about Whitman: "He who read the Iliad, Aeschylus, and Milton and under asclepiadic auspices, in his courage to seek freedom, and with the uprightness of his generous and unaffected nature, Whitman reflects, looking back upon his youth, that he was amazed he had not been crushed by the weight of these powerful masters—although he certainly should be included among the few who might have been crushed."

Ekelund, who was many times on the verge of a breakdown himself, had found that he, a blacksmith's son, in reality had more in common with Whitman than he had with Hölderlin and Nietzsche.

When Ekelund fled Sweden in 1908, it was logical for him to return to Berlin, where he had traveled for the first time in 1902. His letters and notes from Germany speak of his mood and his precarious situation. He writes about the subject of a busy street:

> *The crude street*
> *where unpeaceful, hounded*
> *life is laughing,*
> *crying*
> *cursing*
> *caught in the damned*
> *treacherous simulation*
> *of joy*
> *saw our loneliness*

He also began to doubt that he would continue writing poetry. In preparation—within him as well as on the page—he had works in prose later to be published 1909–1913 under the titles *Ideals of Antiquity, Books and Wanderings, Bow and Lyre,* and *German Vistas.*

In response to a negative comment, Ekelund wrote to his publisher in the form of a funeral invitation (see page 1). The publisher, K. O. Bonnier, was "Invited to honor with his presence . . . Suitable fare will be provided. Guests gather on the border of reason." The handwriting tells of an agitated frame of mind, on the border of breakdown.

To his friend Gustaf-Otto Adelborg Ekelund wrote: ". . . I am thoroughly nauseated with my existence—totally meaningless—a taste of sand . . ."

Later, however, after an interlude in Denmark, he wrote from Kiel: "A grandiose city, the sea is gorgeous, there is a continuous fresh Nordic breeze . . . even the language is utterly gracious . . . spoken with a truly Scandinavian accent."

This mirrors Ekelund's great expectations of finding a large audience on his return to Sweden. But his hopes would be shattered, forcing him into a more cryptic style. The emphasis of the volume presented here is on his writings from the time of his return to his homeland in 1921.

Vilhelm Ekelund's
ESSAYS AND APHORISMS

Ekelund's letter to K. O. Bonnier, 7 April 1906.

The Flowers
of the Destitute
(Books and Wanderings) / 1909

Man's eye for the vain and futile quality of existence is sharpened in a big city. The commotion of hyperactive people chased by work and leisure activities reduces the individual to a mere wave in sunshine falling on the ocean. One day you are gone. Indifferent as if nothing had happened, the ocean murmurs and ripples in accompaniment to the final journey.

Death is everywhere. And all the brutal instincts of that predator provoke him to stalk every miserable moment of life with a force of desperation, to bleed it to the last drop. Death makes man cruel, egotistic, cynical. But its constant presence forces us to ignore it, because everyone knows that he or she who lives, works, and enjoys life as though death never existed is most likely to succeed. The other day there was a terrible accident. A train crashed from an overpass down into the street below, and the mutilated bodies of more than twenty people were pulled out of the rubble. I am traveling the same route by train the following day. The train is packed. It seems we are like cattle herded to the slaughterhouse. The ticket collector's insistent, impatient call: Hurry! Hurry! The frosty sunshine glows blood-red on the tracks polished from constant wear. On the curves the train operator keeps watch, eyes needle-sharp, his face grey and cold. As we pass the site of the disaster, everybody looks down into the depth below and starts talking nervously in hushed voices, "This is where it happened."

This is where it happened! This is the spot! But in the final analysis isn't our whole existence the infamous scene of an accident, the eerie presence of ghosts penetrating the air with their chill?

In a big city the weight of life exerts a heavier pressure on the sensitive mind. Possibilities flash past in a constant stream, faces appear and vanish; for an anguished moment eyes meet, and there is the hint of recognition touching deep down, as if at the fundament of the soul. Then again that notion is lost forever. Eyes constantly meet with the images of misfortune, depravation, vice, and insanity. In the cold of the winter night old, worn men and women hunch in entrances and along the walls of buildings. Their eyes—deep as death—follow the passerby as he hurries among the people suffering constant hunger. He becomes aware of their minds' indescribable anguish, a state of hypochondria bordering on madness, which is the ever present companion of poverty. It seems as though all "higher" more refined suffering of the soul is child's play as compared to this. He sees that depravation, the misery of hunger, is a form of madness, but lacking true insanity's element of healing. Life appears to him as a cursed illness without any remedy, a horrendous never-healing wound, where blood flows black like water from the depth of a contaminated swamp.

Maybe he came from scenic surroundings, where his spirit fortunately thrived, enjoying the gorgeous landscape, the mountains, the ocean, and the air that fortified his mind, made him vigorous and happy in the classical, pagan sense. Images from the bright childhood of humanity were evoked in him. Then he is puzzled by the change that occurs within. What strange, new shades of daylight—heavy and somber! How difficult to defend and protect whatever remains of hope, faith in life, and strength within him—and how close everything dark, resigned, and pessimistic appears!

I have before me a strange book by a man who is a poet of the big city, its philosopher of pessimism like no one else: the writings of Charles Baudelaire, recently published in a complete edition, supplemented with many stray pieces left behind at the deceased man's workplace.

In the tropics there are snakes capable of hypnotizing victims with stares until such prey is sucked helplessly into their jaws. The evil in life had such an effect on Baudelaire. He called his poems *flowers of evil* and that is what they *are*. The misfortune, cruelty, foulness, and delusion of existence never had a keener scrutinizer. And he expressed his observations with an energy possible only in a human who keeps ideals alive in his soul. Productive individuals always demonstrate a strong sensibility to the evil in the character of life. To many the creative spirit is but a means to defend themselves against life, to numb their lack of faith. The strongest ones are probably those who, through the highest possible degree of spiritual enthusiasm, have the strength to elevate themselves to a level where evil to them becomes an indispensable element of existence, a quality essential precisely to produce the type of struggle that gives rise to greatness in humanity.

Struggling against misfortune, pain, despair, the human spirit develops its purest powers, its greatest splendor. Maybe life is something that cannot be defended and perhaps everyone concerned would have been better off without it. Still it is more dignified, more resplendent to walk under the dark iron sky of infinite meaninglessness, than to imagine oneself being a petty object of a mysterious play at blindman's bluff with a final act, the solution of an insipid religious paradise. If God exists, man is ridiculous! Preferable then, is the eternal chill of desolation, the wasteland and the torment—because through them the human being gains greatness. The weak ones—still strong enough to look evil squarely in the eye—submerge themselves defenselessly and unselfishly in the mystery of incurable human misery. They find a strange, painful solace in observing the grotesque relationship between dream and reality, between the heart's urge for refinement and the bottomless crudeness of life. A spiritually radiant world rises out of the deep irony, the soul's first light of dawn. The cruder and more corrupt material desolation becomes, the more audible the delicate rustle of wings seems to grow. Such is Baudelaire's poetry. How could beauty exist except against a background of darkness! It would be as unthinkable as the splendor of the rainbow without the darker backdrop of clouds, which are always there for the deeply sensitive. Who can feel content so long as there exists one single destitute! The person of a higher state of mind must feel agony at heart when confronted with happiness. Too proud to be happy, he or she will regard it as an injustice. The tale about Gautama Buddha and the unfortunate one he meets on his way has a significance of infinite radiance. A man of genius has never escaped the moment when along his way he was forced to kneel before the miserable and thus had to fight for his soul. A true artist is deeply aware in his work of the unfathomable darkness behind everything human. And all joy, all optimism is of no value to spiritual production unless juxtaposed against this ever dark background.

Reading Baudelaire, Fröding[1] often comes to mind. The massive quality of their poetry reveals a closely related sense of life. Life's mass exerts a similar pressure on the heart of each man. Both are of a genius justifying their striving for the ultimate, and thus they are consumed by an overwhelming fire—or neglect it, once kindled. Or perhaps behind it all lies this: they lost faith in their art. They experienced what it means to feel sweetness turn into poison, to sense what was once a blessing become the feeling of a heart sucked by a vampire day and night. The highest was never high enough for them, the most fiery did not have enough fire. It is the nature of the artist to be unable to rest after his accomplishment. He is like the opium addict who, once hooked on the drug, must constantly increase his dose to reach an ultimate high. Bitterly, Baudelaire learned that humanity was least of all inclined to value something as powerful and dense as his poetry. Baudelaire learned what it means to be so careless as to cast roses before swine. Apart from the bright moments in his life made possible by his friendship with Sainte-Beuve, the critic, and Flaubert, the novelist, his later life was one of utter desolation, that of a pariah. As proof, one need only mention that once in a newspaper article he offered his *thanks* to Sainte-Beuve for officially granting him a clean record of character, and conduct as a human. An insult gross enough to kill a horse. The educated populace knows of no sweeter spectacle than the misfortune of a genius. No human instinct functions with a more relentless accuracy than the hatred for everything that contains spiritual greatness and splendor. And for a man of profound knowledge nothing could be wiser than to hide his exceptional character under a mask, with consistency and utmost care. Baudelaire knew too much about human nature, despised its character too much to defend himself. People confronted him with fawning, sympathetic expressions on their faces revealing their preconceived, derogatory opinion of him—and his pride required him

[1] Renowned 19th century Swedish poet.

to strengthen their misconceptions. "The soul of the poet is composed of folly and obstinacy," according to a Chinese saying: "He re-
fuses to enter into explanations with strangers."

Baudelaire was living in Brussels when he was struck by a paralyt-
ic illness. He had left Paris torn by calamities and miseries, faithful
companions of a literary talent set on defying any popular mode of
working. And he had practically given up hope of regaining his spiritual vitality. Great sorrow, misfortune make one prolific and ambitious, force one to think magnanimously of liberation. The pain of
constant needling, the gray everyday pricklings destroy the spirit.
Ennui, hopelessness, "an indolence, the pressure of twenty atmo-
spheres" weighed on his numbed soul. The hypochondria of disease
and poverty spoke out of his words; a total nerve eclipse drove away
the mere thought of work. Lifelong humiliation, hatred, anger, and
hurt pride tore at his heart. By the force of will all poisonous things
can be transformed into balm. Thus, it should be possible to turn
even poverty into something positive. It is not likely to be easy. The
life of a destitute is like living surrounded by mosquitos, gadflies, in-
fested by ticks . . . And woe betide you if your soul has a delicate skin!
Sick, torn to shreds down to his core, lacking the means to pay for
even the most inexpensive doctor's prescription, Baudelaire confronted the horrors of disintegration. His soul was but a wavering
spark over a turbulent sea . . .

Roses for pigs! What terrible blindness my pen conveyed to me as I
wrote those words! As if perhaps poetry were something the world
had no right to despise! Isn't poetry something for the lower classes,
for the failures, the victims of casualties, the poor and hungry? Has
ever a sound, sensible human got the idea of writing poetry? Isn't
poetry something totally opposed to the conventional and fashionable? And the splendor and greatness of the soul, were they ever
accepted by established society? What inexhaustible soundness humanity reveals by its constant rejection of poetry!

Poems are the flowers of the destitutes, the unfortunate ones,
grown far outside orderly society, where good sense, prudence, dullness, and hypocrisy spread with solid opulence. Poetry is something
suspect, worthy of the righteous indignation of any nobly thinking
conservative. Roses for pigs! The swine were annoyed. And rightly
so.

In Memory of
the Centennial of
Edgar Poe's Birth
(Books and Wanderings) / 1909

Today it is a hundred years since Edgar Poe was born. I am sitting in the library at Unter den Linden and have ordered the huge special edition of his writings—a luxury edition for the millionaires of America, printed in 500 numbered copies by Putnam's in New York, shining in gold and white and illustrated with lovely works of art. The writings of Poe, the proletarian, are not available in any complete edition for common mortals. The manuscripts he carried as he wandered starving from newspaper to newspaper along the streets of the big cities, are now within reach of a semieducated dollar mob at inflated prices.—And it would be naïve to let the ways of the world upset you! It would be a naïveté to dream of a different state of things. In reality humanity only has use for the everyday, the "sound," the mediocre,—whoever insists on not conforming to the laws of supply and demand, has no one else to blame but himself—if anybody. Some time ago the millionaire Carnegie expressed concern because Bret Harte's production showed a notable decline in his later days, something that Carnegie attributed to the author's improved living conditions. People who spiritually succumb to opulent living conditions, probably possess insufficient mental capacities at the outset. But in principle Carnegie is right! Kierkegaard would have applauded. The spiritually creative human being is no philistine, no domesticated animal, feeling at home with security and comfort. Generally, he finds such comfort and pleasant laxity revolting—in social as well as in physical life. Whoever regards the need to sustain

himself forever in a powerful, spiritual atmosphere as the most refined enjoyment in life must of necessity strive to reduce comfort to a
minimum. Even Epicurus, the Greek "philosopher of indulgence,"
was a man of strict observance, even of an ascetic character. No work
of genius has been created out of a state of jolly comfort. Struggle is a
necessary ingredient for spiritual production—primarily an inner
one—but there is also an analogue in the outer conditions, which
should not be demeaned as an inspiring force. The creative in spirit
are almost always people who have been prevented from *living* by
both interior and external circumstances working in combination.
Their output is a surrogate for life, never quite capable of filling the
abyss in the human soul. Humanity's greatest spiritual works have
risen out of this disposition, and the philistine does not suspect that
he expresses a deep truth when declaring art a perversity.

Edgar Poe is one of the richest personalities of romantic poetry. He
forces the cultivation of the spiritual visions and the ability to divine
beyond one's senses to some ultimate limit. He elevates pain and anguish to the principle of poetry. People with a creative spirit are those
most likely to discover that beauty thrives preferably in the shadow
of sorrow. And many may have found that from the will, which de-
rives its inspiration from the flexible balancing of this fatally dark
element of beauty, another world of beauty may grow. Perhaps it
doesn't outshine the splendor of the former one, but it is still worthy
of the proud spirit that fears nothing and hopes for nothing. Edgar
Poe is the most radiant being emerging from the domain of pain,
where poetry most often blossoms.

Today, it has become a matter of conscience to many to suspect the
ideal of romantic culture. Whoever looks for arguments to defend a
love not easy to sacrifice, may find in Poe his heart's satisfaction. Poe,
with all the darkness of night, with his embittered and tortured life,
is one of the brightest figures ever to walk the roads of humanity.
While his contemporary spiritual kin, Baudelaire in Paris, Leopardi
in Italy, sank to a level where productivity became an invective and a
jeer aimed at everything and everyone, no power—whether alcohol,
poverty, or death—could destroy the splendor within Poe. There was
in him something that the infamy of the tellurian climate did not affect. With a strange lightness, the hue of rose, everything comes together in him—notwithstanding his intellectual solidity. There is an

atmosphere of the spirit around him. The form of his poem is grand and light at the same time; he is always inspired, and his life seems to exist in a secret relationship with a good genius, with the good forces of life, to which his heart clings. His erotic poetry has that color of rose that makes one think of the cool scent of dew predominant in Greek love poetry. A Swedish literary critic, who had read de Maupassant, recently remarked in an essay about Poe that the erotic motif *was lacking* in his writings. It is as much to the point as it would be to say that Dante in his "Vita Nuova" has shown an astonishing lack of erotic, spiritual imagination. No human ever lived who possessed a greater erotic depth than Poe. His metaphysical view of life has grown out of erotic experience—as the discourse of Plato grew out of Eros.

Of all literary art, Poe values most the lyric poem, an evaluation that weighs rather heavily. It is of little importance if an ordinary writer of verse maintains that his art is of supreme excellence. But Poe is not only a poet writing lyrics of depth and of fiery quality, he is also a master of prose. In comparison few stand up to him. Strindberg, generally and quite rightly, condemns "verse poetry" as the revolting petty art of the "belletrist," but in Poe he would find arguments for the art of verse that he would find hard to reject, and in his own poetry he would find things of a nature he may never have seen before, except in the art of *one man*, his inspiration of later years—Emanuel Swedenborg. Poe has seen the angels of heaven. His soul has drowned in their eyes, he has felt their hair touch his head and he has listened to a melody beyond this world. Few men have had Poe's inspired faith in a good principle of existence. His soul feels inundated by mysterious memories from an obscure past; not for a moment did it occur to him to doubt that this earthly life is but a short stop on an infinite journey, a quick passage across the stage of a great mystery. His rightful home is—*beauty*, goodness.

It is an established fact that a certain superficiality and indifference, or, more bluntly, a convenient portion of stupidity, tends to smooth the road through this vale of tears. Edgar Poe made his living mainly as a literary critic. This tells us something about that profession. A man with his powerful productive source will, only with the greatest difficulty, be able to accommodate himself to the level of the literary critic. A human being who lives culture, as opposed to one who only knows culture, will never be able to communicate in the popular way necessary for a reviewer. A cultural experience can never be expressed in a popular way. Culture is only lived by a few people with a rare spiritual clarity, and it is exactly that *clarity* that appears as the most obscure to the majority of people. A person of a complex nature can hardly imagine finding himself in a more impossible situation than that of a critic. It is in the nature of this spirit to become immediately fascinated by a particular personality's core, which is always behind everything transient and unimportant in the work. This constitutes a secret source of light that imbues everything in the work of art with real life, and allows a personally experienced interpretation. He himself provides the shades and colors by the force of his own intimate life and cultural experiences, rather than giving a flat "analysis" that may satisfy everybody from the standpoint of interest and simplicity. The commonplace writing of reviews is in reality one of the most reprehensible phenomena of modern culture, and it is obvious that productive people of any class never dedicate themselves to this profession. Instead, sterile parasites have seized upon this solution to give the impression of a spiritual life, while lacking any professional proficiency.

Many hypotheses have been presented, most of them deeply naïve, about Poe's alcoholism. It is most plausible that this base profession, that of being a critic, may have played some part. The art of the word was holy to Poe. His style vibrates with the forceful tension of his soul. Each line of his writing is charged with life. It must have been a profanation of the most bitter kind for him to write book reports and reviews—since there is no other name for his critical articles. In this connection he was forced to kill his real self. And what American paper would have accepted Edgar Poe if on each occasion he had spoken from his heart his honest opinion of the literary trash he was forced to write about in a popular vein?

For a man of Poe's spirit, the compromise he had to make, forced by the public's demands, is one of the most destructive of life's humiliations. This compromise required giving up the means of defense that nature had provided his soul to mute despair and the thought of death. It meant separation from all that constituted his good genius. Poe was miserably paid throughout his life because he wrote in a style that was characterized by an American editor as "way over the popular level." Poe was extremely prolific, his works comprise ten considerable volumes. The humiliations he had to suffer were of a kind that one can barely grasp: how was it possible for him to endure life under such terrible pressure? "Among all living, no heart has been more thoroughly abused than mine," he said about himself. His wife's mother walked from newspaper to newspaper with his unsalable manuscripts, begging. His wife died of cold and starvation before his eyes.

Suffering had made Poe ecstatic. In an ecstacy of despair and vision he produced immortal writings during his last years. In his works from these final years there is the tone of rolling thunder against a shore battered by the storms of night.

The inspired human beings, the ecstatic and ambitious ones, most often live under an unbearable pressure. They are *forced* upwards, they thirst for all that is lustrous and powerful in spirit, because only the infinite gives solace to their souls. What is happiness for a man of this kind? Only this: to arrive at the belief that his destiny contains a meaning, to subordinate himself, to deny himself, and to merge with the good. Only through that great love does he become invulnerable. However, in this way he has been *seized* by existence at the foundation of his being, and he has no reproach toward life. Happy, he is not—he is more than that!

Agenda / 1913–1914

p.15,#14   I am but an eye looking into the blind and ghast-
            ly eye of meaninglessness. Why? Who am I? The
            howling loneliness around the human.

p.19,#23 When I was ill this winter I got morphine injections in the evenings.
          In my intoxication I thought of Plato and Emerson with such inti-
          mate feelings, it was as if both were my personal friends, protectors,
          and helpers. This feeling was lovely, I must try never to forget it. The
          reconciliation with life as a whole, which I experienced on these oc-
          casions, should have improved, purified me—
             At the height of one of these happenings I suddenly sensed an an-
          gel bending over my head, and a feeling of heavenly rapture over-
          came me. But then a horrid, devilish monster appeared, and the im-
          age of the angel was torn, vanishing in a wild darkness and
          commotion. Later, at night, I often tried to provoke the angel to reap-
          pear; I never succeeded, but that monster came every night in many
          different disguises.

p.32,#19 Heartbroken by the insults of life.

                    The gallows of Caudin.[1]

                    The Black Hole.[2]

[1]The gallows of Caudin: The Roman army surrounded by the Samnites at the Caudin
Pass had to suffer the humiliation of marching off without clothes and weapons under
a portal or gallows built from lances.
[2]Probably the "Black Hole of Calcutta" where 146 Englishmen were imprisoned after
the fall of the city in 1756; most of them died.

Covered with ice
seeing misunderstanding grow, slander tearing life to pieces, clench-
ing my fists in determined pride . . .

Everything great has already been said. But the person who knows   p.41,#17
how to stimulate his soul with the magnificence of it is always something new.

"Old novelty!"
    But what is genius if not to understand how to make use of past
greatness and the eternally new.

The infidel.   p.47,#4
    Woe to him, who once walked the roads of light and then returned
to the darkness.
See the beautiful world rightly: calm, fast, fleeting. Angel of victory.
Deign to come near me. May I be seized by the storm once and for all.
Redeem my heart, loosen my tongue.

What the ancient philosophers called "the sublime good" is still the p.47,#5
guiding star of all culture. The independence of the spirit—the value
of life. The substance of the whole journey on earth is to long for this
destination; because you never arrive. What does this inescapable
need of freedom imply?

One ought to concentrate on all that's primitive and fresh in the lan- p.48,#7
guage with a boundless avarice. No other words should be recognized than those **strikingly fragrant**. The ones smelling of the sea
are the best. If you have the right vernacular you have the right philosophy.

To see: the source of the heroic. For him who sees truly, sharply, and p.48,#8
profoundly the world dissolves into light.

Only he who can forget himself has strength. Bakunin.   p.49,#10
    That is the egotism of wisdom: to burn all that is pettily, painfully,
stupidly selfish in the fire of love of spiritual vision and freedom; to
live and not to live. In toto: the intoxication is a necessity. True life is
to be swept away by it. The outer world must be detached; it must not
cling.

p.58,#2 Dostoevski raging over the Germans makes me happy. He detests Berlin.

Dark and dangerous forces have started to throw their shadows over me these days. How I fear this state of mind! At any price I have to keep connections open to the good powers that came to me during my illness. The slightest breeze from the desolation of the time before makes me shudder.

p.69,#30 The description of a piece of art must in itself be a piece of art; this comes as naturally to me as the fact that the painting of a landscape or of a human being has to be art. This of course also goes for the description of a book, of an author, the so-called critic.

p.72,#6 Bakunin's words about the strength in forgetting one's self are forever noteworthy! To be faithful; faithfulness to the cause. The only road to what is just, to liberation from all petty coquettishness, fits of temper, personal indulgence; the only road to a great, simple style. What absurdity for a grain of dust in the ocean of life to want to be personal! If there is any bliss, any satisfaction to be found for this speck of matter, it must be in becoming a clear eye, unselfish, contemplative, gratefully loving, losing itself in limitless love. You are a victory yourself within the eternal victory Life, if your eye is clear.

p.74,#9 The strong is always classic. Whoever, blinded by Nietzsche, calls Schopenhauer romantic, will soon have to relearn. It would be just as well to call Strindberg a romantic.

p.80,#24 I note again and again that an angry nervousness follows as a reaction to my relief and joy of a success, a fortunate event. It's no doubt a bad character symptom. "We others are happy when we get money—you get mad," said L., reproachfully.

p.81,#27 That the joy of success, of being in favor with the world, is a weak, confused, unworthy state of mind has always been my firm conviction. When in such a mood—it would be inhuman to be free of it— my nerves yearn for the desolate and austere.

p.82,#29 The unreflected enthusiastic faith in the magically suggestive power of the word does not possess me any more. In its place has come a certain (sound) apprehension of everything ambitiously nervous. Does there exist for me a road to the love of clarity without any sidelong glances of foolish egotism? Watch the stars. Their gaze can cool a human heart.

A year ago illness struck me morally and intellectually unprepared. That was the most difficult part of my misfortune, hardest to overcome. I was ashamed, deeply humiliated. How different things would have turned out, if my mind had been pure.

As far as our concept of animals and plants goes, future man will probably regard us as savages. That man is a kind of animal is now an acknowledged fact; to me it is natural to look upon certain animals as—humans. The dog is mostly a child. The horse often has the expression of a human, utterly weary of life. p.83,#12

The individual in plants and animals will probably be an important field of research for future man. A mighty tree, which among ordinary specimens had exceptional size and perfection, was looked upon with reverence and religious feeling by ancient man. And the direction of the future will point toward the "primitive," the instincts and divinations of prehistoric times; (Lessing[1] applies this in regard to metempsychosis). p.84,#3–7

When reading Humboldt[2] a few years ago, I was struck by this thought. The oak tree contains a profound culture symbol; the Germans still describe its leaf as heroic; the color of bronze in the autumn. The life of a tree is admirable and joyous. There are trees individualized to a greater or lesser extent.

In an epigram of Greek origin a walnut tree complains about how the boys knock down its fruits and hurt it by throwing stones at it.

The maple resembles a Nordic woman, but its relative the platan is Greek, a masculine gentle genius. In Vienna I saw a platan with a great resemblance to Sophocles or Plato. The German tree is naturally the linden; it seldom has a stately posture, but in its youth it has a certain tender charm, bordering on gracefulness; in this way it resembles the German woman. The beauty in a German—when it is

[1] 18th century German writer and critic, the foremost German representative of the Enlightenment.
[2] Alexander von Humboldt, German natural scientist.

there at all—lies precisely within that realm: in existing on the verge of gracefulness. Exactly by not embodying the fulfillment of grace it reminds one always of spouting with its everlasting budding beauty.

The wretched parodies of pine trees around Berlin look like bookish, Prussian schoolteachers of the pseudo-Germanic type with filthy, yellowish beards and piggish, pimpled faces. I saw such a tree that clearly wore spectacles.

Prehistoric man conceived the trees in a more dignified, humane way than we do; the Greeks did so intimately, with friendship. How vulgar our nature-sentimentality appears compared with their childlike, fresh concept.

Apollo, no doubt, was honored with the laurel because of this way of experiencing the tree as a personality in the inner vision of men of divination. The tree is older than the principle, more ancient than Apollo himself!

p.86, Cassianus: "*De coinobiorum institutis*."[1] The so-called Middle Ages had
#10–12 brilliant psychologists.

A refined will of power—rather than fear of hell—

Raw joy causes the inner horizon to shrink, sorrow enlarges it.

My best frame of mind: the rare moments when I looked in wonder and compassion at small-minded, miserable, evil people—and without any hatred. After such experiences I was overcome by fear, flung back into violent and bitter affectations, and could perhaps sense something like the same fear as someone on the verge of going blind.

If I want to say the right things, I must speak in a subdued voice.

The medieval fear of hell, its burden of sin, religious desperation, all the depressions that people had to struggle against, must have been compensated by the certainty of man's individual immortality.

There was much philosophic ambition beneath the religious asceticism.

When a person, sensitive by nature and circumstance, becomes the object of public attention, thus exposed to uninterrupted falsifi-

[1] Johannes Eremita Cassianus (360–435?), one of the first founders of monastic institutions in Western Europe. His work "De coinobiorum institutis" (Twelve books) describes monastic life.

cation, misinterpretation, envy, slander, etc., his only rescue is—swiftness.

The world is no other than yourself. He who has reason to be disgusted by himself certainly has cause for despising the whole world. Your most terrible enemy is yourself. Keep the peace! Keep the peace!

"World history" is but an intermission in an ice age episode. The intellect wants to murder the heart, but has a bad conscience. When you are terribly irascible, painfully sensitive to stupidity, slander, and injustice, it is truly the greatest misfortune to also be heavy, stiff, inflexible. Then you are in immediate danger of suffocating. It is possible to find joy under a sky of ever-amassing dark clouds: provided you are the storm. Thus Strindberg was happy.

I close the year by being appalled that I am not appalled. p.89,#20

I began reading books of natural science which had a calming effect on me.

The donor of blood, the original one, will rarely harvest, but walks through life a suspect individual. Then comes the parasite, that is to say the "critic," the discoverer, the literary historian; he will become a man of high repute, professor of the rags of a genius' lifelong misery.

—Accumulate to become a sun—before the dark overwhelms you. p.92,#28 Only he can bear death who at the core of his being is all sun. That's the sense of Goethe's "*entelechia.*"[1] If this faith is a dream, it is a strong and powerful dream that you can live by.

Right to life: by the power of one's will to become sun.

Thirsting for life, feeling yourself wrinkling, withering away: you hate the sun.

> *Tristi fummo Nel aere dolce che dal Sol s'allegra Portando* p.97,#1
> *dentro accedioso fummo.*[2]

[1]A Greek term used by Goethe in the concept of soul.
[2]Dante places low in the Inferno those who willfully live in sadness . . . "beneath the dreary marsh lie those who were sullen in the sweet air, saying for ever and ever through their sighs: "Tristi fummo . . ."" (Oscar Wilde).

When I first came upon these lines of Dante in his "Inferno," many years ago, hardly more than a child, I felt strangely moved by them. I sense a vital importance in them; a divination that Dante here touches upon the roots of human evil itself, the original sin of the wretched—heirs of the Sun and Eternity.

p.97,#2 Don't forget that to read is a sedative and like all such drugs dangerous. The more you read, the more you have to write! and see to it that you keep agile and fit. Nietzsche finds it a sin to read before noon . . . *"in der Morgenröthe seiner Kraft"* (in the dawn of one's powers).

p.106,#6 Today the seagulls sat in a crowded, motionless flock on the ice of the lake sunbathing. From the distance it looked like a vast island of white buttercups.

  Is not "altruism" the highest potency of the will for power? Fichte makes out of Alexander the martyr of an idea. You can't help smiling. Why not just as well Napoleon? Is it any better to sacrifice oneself for the Macedonian than for the French *"gloire"*?

p.123,#9 Once the first week of April had passed, all the crows left the park, after having frequented it "en masse" during winter. They moved to the country. What sophisticated beasts! I feel an intense urge for wide open spaces, the sky, horizons. Now I miss the healthy, honest, coarse cawing and the bland chirping of the small birds makes me sick.

p.133,#14 I'm astounded by the human grace, the childlike innocence, the childish soul of the globeflower (Trollius europaeus). I won't ever forget the strong impression this flower made upon me as a child, the mystic enchantment it evoked in my mind, and as I look at it now, this day in May, I have the same feeling.

  In French it's called "ball of gold" (*boule d'or*), but the Swedish "meadow ball" (*ängsboll*) is more beautiful.

p.134,#15 This frantic tempo of the first and finest of summer! Before you know it, it's gone.

  And this is life. What's the use despairing. You can't keep anything. Everything declines steeply into the dark.

Went on passing through the land of gorgeous scenery. p.138,#2
There was summer on all roads, and the dogs thrust their tongues out.

Today is a king in disguise.

This life full of death—this death full of life. p.140, #10–11
Augustinus

In the morning I built myself an altar, at night I demolished it. Anxiety, anxiety. And today is perhaps the most beautiful day of the year . . . wind and glow of June, as though the angels of the sky fanned the air with their wings. How this beauty punishes me! And nevertheless it was the most innocent joy that was the source of this agony.

I have noticed that precisely such days often follow upon devastating nights. I've seen others on similar days suffer the same agony, while I myself was in high spirits, and nothing else has caused me to feel such deep compassion. I was terrified they would notice my happiness, the airy, light freshness of my spirit, and I distorted the features of my face, walked heavily, stooped my back, so as not to hurt them. May that be to my credit! Let it alleviate my anxiety now.

Nordic and Classic / 1914

p.29,#13[1] Beauty in your life, beauty in your death, beauty in Gehenna . . . only, only by tumbling into the flame of a thought, a dream, a phantasma.

p.37,#29 The Germans are the modern revivers of paganism. The intensity in their hatred of Christianity has no equal in any other nation in the world. Thor with his hammer has risen again in Dühring, in Nietzsche. Hammer! No, here we have that huge, thundering sledge hammer . . .

Get rid of the disgusting state-Christianity, mass secession from the national church! It is a joy to see with what enthusiasm and fire a Berlin mob can be swept away by an ardent oration against that highly comfortable fop-religion to which the honest, dark, radical pessimism of the noble Nazarene has been degraded. Perhaps it would warm his heart if he could rise from the dead and see the hate blaze in these people's eyes. He who raged against "the world," against the philistinism, the halfheartedness and the lack of ideals— if he had guessed that he was forging a weapon for the hands of exactly "this world . . ." He who sensed the misfortune of humanity so deeply, that he didn't find any other solution to its enigma than to entirely reject and turn his back on all that is earthly, would see his name dragged into the service of an intense philistine optimism . . .

[1]The pagination refers to the reprint of "Nordic and Classic" in *Dagbok och Diktverk* by Sven Linqvist, published by Bonniers, Stockholm, 1966.

Whoever comes to a standstill, imagines that he has been deserted by his genius. There is something to that. The genius of life spares the swift ones. They have no pangs of conscience, but burn odds and ends in their own flame, instead of heaping things around them like the hypochondriacs. p.40,#38

Life's foulness and repulsiveness have the adventurous character of a fairy tale for he who keeps his aim high. The secret is to create as great a contrast as possible. Thus the ugly is valued; draws the string of the bow, tightens the string of the lyre. Ugliness is ugly only to the flaccid ones. p.43,#48

It is strange how even the thought that the greatest is futile can give strength and height to the soul. p.44,#52

The Jesuit principle: withdrawal from the world—in order to act on the world—was frequently also the principle of genius. p.44,#53

Faith makes alive, that is to say makes life worth living. p.44,#54

The ideal gives the most ardent intoxification: swiftness, forgetfulness, potent calm. Faith in beatitude makes the feeble of heart lionhearted. p.44,#55

Freedom is worth suffering for. If you have looked down upon those who have chosen to join the ranks of the social animals; don't get envious, when they are at ease while you anguish. p.45,#56

The essence of hypochondria is often plainly an oversight of the importance of keeping a well-balanced tension between need and satisfaction. Oh, these deeply romantic emotional diseases. p.45,#57

Whoever can journey away from his anguish is blessed; the bliss of the productive one. By means of his work he puts continents and oceans between himself and his miseries. p.49,#65

Success and security often instigate doubt in one's own spiritual strength, an inclination to be content with the thoughts of others. To p.49,#66 be placed on treacherous ground, in whatever sense, is good; generally you learn to stand on your own feet only when the ground is rocking under them.

p.50,#67 Humor.
In *Confession*, Gogol speaks of violent attacks of melancholy, which he cannot explain to himself. To relieve himself of the insufferable pressure, he invents ridiculous characters, acting to himself, playing to ease his anguish. He invents his novel as anybody else travels the world, and takes his hypochondria for long walks. He makes up his book—without any literary intent—to simply distract his own mind. Thus the intimate delight of his works; the childlike quality that you find in Cervantes, to whom he is closely related.

p.50,#68 "Poverty is an endlessly long night," says some knowing man. No, he didn't know the poor! It's a day, unfortunately: an endless, painful day with a sharp and piercing light, that smarts in the eyes, like glowing needles in the soul . . . In Scania[1] one says about somebody utterly impoverished, that he "neither sees nor hears" from poverty. Greek poets have expressed themselves word for word in the same manner. The matter goes deep and has an awesome reality. Utter destitution is a type of hypochondria that borders on insanity. The more dignified agony of the soul can be child's play compared to the soul—suffering such simple people endure.

p.51,#71 To be consistent can sometimes be easy enough. To be honestly inconsistent can be more difficult.

p.52,#73 Humiliation, hurt pride, the choked heart's desire—all good things: inflammatory, re-creative. But God's mercy on whoever has to live on pepper and salt alone!

p.52,#75 The artist and the poet have the facility for mistaking pure languor for meditative peace and strength. True meditation "rests" in swiftness.

[1] Province in southern Sweden.

A cat that has drunk vinegar cannot make a face more comic than the p.52,#76
editorial writer hurting on behalf of the literary honor of the nation,
when he expresses his regrets on products of the spirit that cannot be
filed in the large category of sound, patented harmlessness.

A book—glimmering from fire and salt—should be like a good p.55,#82
storm, continual, powerful, ceaseless, with a deep murmur as night
falls.

Nothing is more humiliating than the foolish indignation one senses p.55,#83
after having left the company of people whose conversation has
been raw, poor, and limited. How many have the strength and vision
to recognize what is most pure and real within us in the midst of life's
platitudes! The greatest achievement in this context—and one has
every reason to congratulate oneself on having come this far—is
generally to keep silent, which Schopenhauer recommends as the
only solution.

A muggy summer evening on the train. He has deep dark wrinkles p.55,#84
around rigid, heavily staring eyes; his face covered with sweat and
dirt. He is coming from work in one of the northern suburbs of Berlin, on his way home to the dark hole at the end of a back courtyard
on Ackerstrasse. Well-dressed people, traveling third class out of
miserliness, are seated around him. A gentleman enters the train at a
station, an executive, a businessman, or the like. The educated, kind
expression on his face suddenly becomes one of deep disgust and reproach, when he sees that all seats are taken except for one next to
the poorly dressed man. And with a gesture, as if it were a question of
sitting down in a bed of nettles, he finally takes the seat, after due
consideration.

The scene was ugly, even in indescribably ugly Germany.

But I happened to think of one or two other things dulling my indignation.

Man is such a coward that an exceptionally high degree of education is necessary in order to dare to appear in the company of a
poorly dressed person (that is, unless one is not entirely protected by
social standing, wealth, etc.). The more refined human being, who
catches himself unprepared in a similar situation, is painfully sur-

prised and consoles his conscience by blaming such action on the general stupidity of society, of which he as well as others is a victim. But in the end the cowardice and shabbiness remain, no less disguised.

p.56,#85 The noise from the street under my window rarely bothers me. But once every week in the evening—summer evenings around six o'clock—I hear from down there a sound that is hard for me to listen to: the streetsweepers on Saturday night. All the anguish of homelessness rises in me at that sound.

p.56,#86 To be wealthy and misanthropic is all very well. Schopenhauer flourished marvelously in his contempt of the world. But beware of being contemptuous of man, you penniless wretched creature . . . the roads you walk are red hot.

p.56,#89 Once Emerson, Amiel, Nietzsche had discovered the great poem, can anybody any longer take "lyrics," this art of the intellectually impotent, seriously?

p.63,#104 Will ever the mediocre and tepid, the feeble super-sensitive-minded, cease to be labeled as aristocratic . . . and the strong and fiery as something plebeian? What grossness Dostoevski had to endure! And until his last breath—Strindberg—who eventually was given the formal stamp certifying that he was a "noble man."

Spiritus magnificentia: I believe that is Quintilianus' characterization of Pindar's style, but I would rather have it attributed to Goethe; even to Strindberg, who in his old age developed a great similarity to Goethe (if one can speak of "old age" in the case of Strindberg). Goethe remarked that he had always kept positive action before his eyes, and shoved aside everything polemic, negative. That was easier for him than for Strindberg. But in spite of all—toward the end, he too, becomes magnificent like Goethe. To be able to focus eyes and heart on the holy cause without any hesitation, while enduring the shower of stupidity and grossness (never was Strindberg as persistently needled as during his last days) gave a majestic tone to his voice.

There's the fine thought expressed by Burns (and Maeterlinck; yes, p.63,#105
you find it as far back as Angelus Silesius) that man is God to the dog.
The dog gets his God for free, but not so man! That is the awkward,
and productive side of man.

The greatest moment: Like the silent interplay of shadows in a bud- p.63,#106
ding forest—the silence of a thought's interacting shadows extend-
ing inside me.

The same goes for hatred as for other passions: only lifting them to p.64,#110
spiritual height gives redemption. For the swift ones the passion is
both nonexisting and existing at the same moment. That's good,
sound fervor! When lifting hatred to a high level, it vanishes, becomes something else.

Into the dog's sense of life enters, no doubt as an essential fact, the joy p.66,#117
that God created so many trees and lampposts for him to lift his hind
leg against. If the literary critic's psyche could be analyzed, one
would surely find there a vital, analogous disposition: the happiness
that God, among the mass of harmlessly acceptable authors, created
also the "curious" and original, unacceptable ones, for the critic to
rush up to and lift his leg against.

When it became fashionable to acknowledge him, they came rush- p.67,#118
ing . . . then, dismayed, he turned from them, that ungrateful ego-
tist.

Maybe some authors, sentimental in a better sense of the word, have p.71,#124
a task to perform, which should not be looked down upon: they can
be enjoyed by narrow-minded, rough people, for whom it's good to
have their inner life touched a bit now and then in order to get an idea
of how real people feel . . . For an easily moved person of an inflammatory, higher nature it is a perversion to read such books, and in
youth, clearly damaging.

Hatred can be penetratingly keen-sighted, but never in the fullest p.74,#130
sense; only love has horizon.

p.74,#132 Ill-humor: from narrow-mindedness, from lethargy. Anger is a different matter.

p.76,#139 He lived for so long with enthusiasm and beauty that he found living so a matter of course; and he thought this could never be taken from him. Then he became careless, began to neglect that lovely fire, and one ugly day it was extinguished.

p.78,#147 To be salt, to be fire is to live. All else is death. One finds it interesting, creditable, yes, even tragic to have lost faith in life, but that is as uninteresting as rotten fish.

Veri Similia / 1915–1916

Dostoevski

Whoever carries the urge for truth in his heart can never be said to be p.11,#I unhappy in the common sense of the word. But there are some words by Shakespeare that perhaps throw more light on the evolution of man's urge for truth than any other phrase I have read. He talks about "scaring Satan by speaking the truth" (Henry Percy in *Henry IV*, part I). For some men truth came to light—for the majority truth is a big empty word, the object of lifeless respect—thanks to that very fact that they had "Satan" riding them. They made virtue out of the necessity, and such virtue is the strongest, says Shakespeare. In suffering is the great consolation that within it grows the urge for truth—just as someone ill with a high fever can keep his will to live alive with his thirst, fantasizing for nights and days on end about a lovely spring in the woods by his distant childhood home— or a row of horses drinking from an old trough outside the stables. Much in Dostoevski's writings tells about an urge for truth of that nature. Occasionally a breed of people existed that could not be called "good" in the common sense; where the urge to transform their lives into truth was strong and for whom that fresh spring flowed more generously than for others—precisely because of their ardent thirst.

Whoever has the ability to deny pain and fear becomes God, says Kirilov in *The Demons*. p.15,#IV

Through suffering to ecstasy: that is the road trodden by all great mysticists, Dostoevski as well as Nietzsche. Should one believe Dostoevski's heart to be richer and wiser than Nietzsche's? Was it his wisdom to be weak, gentle; and a sign of narrowness, impoverishment, when Nietzsche wanted to be strong, hard? It is not a question of superiority nor inferiority. Both were close to life; both chose roads leading to what is real, to religion and high spirits. But in this extraordinary situation which is to live, does it really seem right for a human, wanting to be hard? Isn't the whole attitude of Dostoevski more humane? Isn't it just improbable that the spirit of man, and then embodied by its noblest bearers, should have walked so far down the detour of sorrow, if that would have been out of the way in a real sense. This recondite urge indicates a concealed relationship between sorrow and the strength of true joy, because human genius aims with necessity and basically at expansion, the amplification of the power of joy, at the discovery and conquest of the possibilities of life, courage, happiness. One commits the sin of being naïve when charging "Pessimism;" the same empty-headedness as the peasant who simple-mindedly came dragging firewood to the stake of the religious reformer.

p.31,par 2   Interest in Dostoevski is constantly growing in France and Germany. It may be of significance that Germany is the later of the two to grant him admission among its idols and "*Erlöser.*"[1] Or isn't the innermost principle of the new Germany to be the stronghold against Asiatic forces, the obscure powers of undisciplined sentimentalism lacking both style and direction, call it Christianity or nihilism. Note the words of Bismarck: "There are male and female nations; the Russians (and the Danes) belong to the latter!" When Dostoevski on his travels was forced to go through Berlin, he fell into a state of fury, which very nearly caused him to have a stroke. And how he gnashed his teeth while in Dresden, Baden-Baden; how he frets in his novels; how he comes down upon the Germans like thunder out of the Old Testament in his letters. And there are numbskulls who doubt the hate between nations, who imagine that today's wondrous means of communication have brought people too close to each other not to realize that we are all brothers. Yes, "today's communications" have

[1]Redeemers

brought men close to each other, as close as steel and flint can learn to know each other, before they ignite the flame. Whoever has heard Russians talk about Germans, Germans about Russians, will have had strange things disclosed to him, things that lie beyond Bismarck's simplification.

From the early letters, most of them to his brother, you still get no p.34,par 2 sense of the poet in Dostoevski, the fate of man in him. He is open, cheerful; at the age of twenty-five he has his great literary success; lives impassionately, works fervently. It is 1846, the year Gogol renounces himself as an author: in *Correspondence with Friends*, and in *Confession*, the writings that so strangely foreshadow the advent of Tolstoy. He burns his manuscripts: they contain nothing of real use to humanity; a writer should not work solely for the satisfaction of taste and intellect, he is obliged before God to serve his fellow man, direct, advise, give consolation. Man's destiny is to serve. Gogol's grand literary ambition and great triumph deeply engage the young Dostoevski. That he should rather starve than write some "*invita Minerva*,"[1] stands clear to him. At the same time he made the acquaintance of the 25-year-old Turgenev, and the delight was mutual. Then comes the great catastrophe, imprisonment and deportation, the long terrible road from hypochondria to epilepsy, ending in Semipalatinsk, where, he himself diseased, marries a sickly woman. Dostoevski would surely never have become merely a good writer, a good *belletrist*, but there is little doubt that the catastrophe has been of some help to him. In an introspective as well as an external sense it throws him out of the insipid and narrow atmosphere of literary circles, which didn't suit his grand nature; it forces him up against his moral resources, the fresh depths, where the essence of life is determined. And he became one of those, "who walked the vale of tears creating there founts."

An utterance of Soloviov moves him deeply: "Humanity knows p.39,par 1 much more than it is able to express."

—There is something in the character of Dostoevski that might be called the cunning of goodness.

[1] Repugnant to Minerva (Roman goddess of the liberal arts, etc.).

p.42,par 1 Michelangelo walked "as alone as the executioner" obsessed by his
p.43,par 2 monopoly craze. . .

Eventually joy is what most "mysticists," that is to say, philosophers concerned with life, ponder more than anything. Joy is what is
true, devout, real. That's the way Goethe felt, who really becomes a
mysticist through his so-called faith in reason. That is the nectar of
the flower of world culture. In his time, Emerson may have been the
most fortunate gatherer of this honey. He knew the art of being
still, understood it as Meister Eckhart did. "All right thought is devout." In our day when everything has turned to public rivalry, this
strength is so rare. The Muse of reason is pushed out on the street to
make money. Should one strive for humility and quiet thought, this
is done only with the purpose of hitting a competitor over the head
with one's own virtue. When Strindberg became wise and gentle,
then in all earnestness he began tearing people to pieces. Wisdom
in itself wasn't payment enough, unless he had an absolute monopoly on the status of being wise. Not only the weak suffer from this
monopoly ailment, a very unphilosophical disease; many strong
people suffer from it as well. But was it then too much to ask, that this
extraordinary man wanted his monopoly? But that is exactly it: that
is was *not* too much. It was the least and the most stupid that he
could ask for.

p.44,par 1 There is a border line, beyond which joy sinks to false security and
contentment, loses its airy and delicate dissatisfaction.

The compulsion of spiritual animation should never be felt any
heavier than a frail hand touching your shoulder. For the poet, a
forced effort seldom gives birth to anything but falsification. And it
cannot be different for the thinker. Whatever good that was thought,
happened without effort. To sense the truth is the art of being still.

p.44,par 3 "*Sine ira et studio.*"[1] Unless you get truth as a gift, you'll never get it.
Does one notice any forced effort in Goethe? It is this wondrous fact,
the quiet, fast, fleeting state of Goethe, which has been captured in
the word "Olympic." Confront any of the great modern culture workers with this and he will deflate to respectable mediocrity. Goethe

[1]Without anger and predilection (Tacitus' *Annals*).

called himself a dilettante. One who made no fuss, who understood the art of stillness. In Goethe's case we can most certainly talk about laziness, without being paradoxical. Can there be any effort in sublimity and happiness? The diligence of laziness is the best diligence.

The face of life.
He came home in a blessed mood, having wandered with fresh and p.51
beautiful thoughts, believing he was fully reconciled with life. With light steps he mounted the stairs intending to continue shaping graceful thoughts in the night's stillness. When suddenly he heard a scream; its tone so terrible it seemed beyond the limits of the human voice, as though it rose out of the inner depths of life, of hell. A woman came rushing, falling, rolling, tumbling down the stairs . . . a woman who, an instant ago, had seen her child fall through a high window in the building. That night he wrote nothing about the atonement of life in thought.

Whoever lives for a long time in a foreign country, would, it seems, p.75,#18
eventually enter into a sweeter love relationship with his native tongue than anyone else. To him the language finally becomes like a dream, a world on the other side of the world, a horizon beyond reality. He might come to see the language: visualize it with something of that dark force with which he glimpses the earth of his childhood home, see it with his entire body, as though ripped apart by the force of that sight.

To read a great author with a sizeable production is like traveling in a p.77,#23
big country. You are thrown about, hit by a tumultuous barrage of rapidly changing impressions. One day you decide for sympathy, another for antipathy toward a country you really understand nothing of as yet. Eventually you learn to know it. Then the lesser impressions of dislike and admiration evaporate, and there remains an all encompassing living fact, which causes one's inner horizon to grow, assume outlines, and expand: as at the end of summer when hot air recedes and a strong northwestern wind makes the landscape show a suggestive face, which you never suspected in the muggy heat of summer.

p.78,#25 The Baltic Sea's most gorgeous day in German poetry glows out of Fehmarn and Kiel, by Klaus Groth; from Rügen and Stralsund, by Ernst Moritz Arndt. Goethe never saw the Baltic.

Arndt has virtually turned Rügen into an Ithaka of the Baltic; the seventy-year-old man's tales from his childhood are among the loveliest to be found in German letters, not even surpassed by Gottfried Keller in *Der grüne Heinrich*, which are of the same spirit. We Swedes have let this classic work pass unnoticed *Erinnerungen aus dem äusseren Leben*, even though it's written by a man of Swedish ancestry, born in a Swedish province, and in spite of the fact that it spans the most magnificent bridge between the Swedish and the German. The great race-apostles write mountains of books about what "Germanic" means. But if you look them in the mug, you'll find they look like mongols themselves. Real people of race are not at all that shrewd. They present us the living fact in its quality of pure human personality and poetry. Arndt is this kind of man; and those who live to see will surely experience again the emergence of that type after the new era of blood, and the fate it may bring Germany.

Don Quixote.

p.83 When I was very young and hardly realized how controversial a work this was, I was already disturbed by it.

An inspiration that's almost criminal! exclaims Barbey d' Aurévilly.[1] An insult to tradition, heckling of enthusiasm, of Christian compassion, woman worship, the poetry of exaltation; the work of an old geezer! An elder who makes fun of his youth, senses the prosaic in his century rise around him *"comme une glaise froide qui commence à prendre sa poitrine et qui va bientôt l'étouffer."*[2] Voltaire was the one who took up this piercing heckler's hiss a century later in *Candide*. Cervantes is the greatest melancholic of all Europe's humorists. *"Sublime tristesse!"*

Candide and—*"Sublime tristesse . . ."* If one were to believe in this melancholy, Don Quixote would be a disguised defense for the exaltation, and d'Aurévilly's indignation would be unfounded.

That an old man, and a southerner like Cervantes, would have in-

[1] French novelist (1808–1889)
[2] "like cold mud starting to grip his chest soon to suffocate him."

dulged in such a desperate irony seems quite unlikely. He was too wise a man and too good a poet. He had more opportunities to endure the violent variety of this world's evil than most reasoners and moralists, and was surely therefore less thin-skinned than these gentlemen. And he had a surer eye than the philosophers for the images of life, their freshness and their fullness of character in moments of affliction as well as in moments of delight. Maybe the plain fact is that his intentions are reasonably "serious" in both directions: in their melancholy—it certainly isn't sublime, rather on the dry side—concerning the tragedy of the human heart and thought in a know-all world, as well as in his reserve toward this infatuation. This is an attitude that might ask: is the human predicament worthy of the grand and serious gestures, is it fitting for as wretched a creature as man to take himself seriously?

When the last philosopher made his entry into the asylum and his eyes fell on the row of physicians and attendants, he smiled benignly to them all and said: "*Ich danke für das grossartige Empfangen.*"[1] This scene might come to mind, when Don Quixote marches into the "citadel," to be dubbed a "knight" by an innkeeper and a couple of whores, and to "guard arms" while the donkey drivers sit and grin at him from the windows.

Halcyon.

Summer dominates Nordic poetry, quite naturally. The great beauties of winter have seldom been given justice. Strangely enough it seems that the poet never paid attention to the extraordinary days of winter solstice, the so-called halcyon days. Those dark-golden days of grandeur when the horizon widens, the surface of the sea ripples, and the movement of the waves has the sound of summer, and suddenly islands become visible that have been hiding under the horizon since the first days of fall frost. In the middle of the day there is a mild, warm semidarkness like the dusk of a midsummer evening. p.90

How great the symbol in the ancient poem: the symbol of sorrow for victory. Halcyon, the strange bird, nests on the naked sea during these short days of peace. The great spirits are the halcyon days in the life of humanity. The winter storm of existence surrenders to the

[1] "I thank you for the grand reception."

spirit that creates and gives birth during a few short days while light and darkness struggle. The sea obeys, and the continuance of the rare species is secured.

p.93 *The day.*

The day is a prince in disguise.

The art of living: to honor the day.

Life is so cunning that we let it slip through our hands by mere indisposition and absentmindedness. There is always something to be attended to first, cleared out of the way; always some other day that will stand out as real, and never the present one, which only is a simple ordinary day . . .

On that morning when I rise for the first time after an illness and see the sea and the hills of the islands shine through the blossoming poplars of the garden in the solar wind, I learn more than my studies could ever teach me. There is a phrase by Montesquieu that I love second to none: "I wake every morning with a secret joy of perceiving the light; I see it in rapture as it were."

p.96 When the young Wesley[1] ransacked his heart, he found that his Christianity was but a "cute summer religion." For winter and storm and death it was useless.

That's how things stand with our highly praised culture, our urge for "self-refinement," our "love of truth;" it's all a slight summer philosophy. A gust of wind is all that's needed to bring down the whole house of cards—a glance from someone on the street, a smile that might occur suspect to you, a word whispered behind your back . . . not to speak of storm and death. Our philosophy is in no way sufficient to dampen the pains of plain ordinary irritability, and irascibility. It's excellent for the after-dinner drink and the cigar, sure!

It's always a question of need! Changing around the old proverb one might say: a book that stands up in need is a book indeed. Yes, one might think it over more than once, before one seriously wishes to be placed in such situations and such moods of life, where a book becomes its full reality, becomes something that enters the bloodstream. One may find it desirable or not, but the truth is, that any other way of reading is like a child playing with a knife.

[1]Founder of a religious sect (1703–1791).

Se tu segui tua stella.[1]   p.112,#7

The great distinction: in every age there were some who dedicated their lives to following their genius; most people followed only their own bodies to the grave. There exists a fine dust in life that is stealing life from us. The best men have come close to the secret of that dust. For them there was no choice. Only this: If you don't want to take the best, you have to take the muddiest road. For most people there exists a third alternative, which is sufficiently good and acceptably shabby, neither entirely one nor the other. At best they dispose of the whole matter with a certain self-contempt that to them is a kind of narcotic. Not so the exceptional man. It is his own mysterious, unexplorable, secretly manifest genius that life must make him aware of in order that he may not perish and become the most desolate of all. What is "genius?" Awareness of one's secret instinct and trusting to it, more than to anything others say and have said. *Nunc parvulos nobis dedit igniculos (natura)*[2] *(Tusculan Disputations,* 3.1). This light, these odors traversing the soul, are in the end the most real and the strongest things in our beings, frailer than cobweb, stronger than iron, persisting and saving us when everything collapses, the only things that make a fate beautiful and meaningful.

What does the sea say? Is there something pagan about the sea? p.111,#6
Why does one despise all subtle pedants when looking at the sea? Why can Kierkegaard have no part in it?

And yet . . . no. Great thought, classicism and strength call for a pure heart, and so does paganism and the pagan quality of the sea. What is sound is just. Christian thought, or romantic thought, whatever one may call it, has a right to live, too; and life needs both— needs the sick as well as the strong. He is noble who does justice to both. The great dramatists have had a finer feeling for these things and a more refined need for justice than the moralists.

Amor dei[3]—Heraclitian, Spinozan, Fichtean, or Nietzschean—no! I don't believe that any man has ever been able to transform this into his own blood. This place of life has its *genius loci*[4], but a genius with

[1]If you follow your star (Dante).
[2]Now nature gave us little sparks of fire.
[3]Divine love (in a Heraclitian, Spinozan sense).
[4]The genius of the place.

two faces: one of morning, the other of evening, and philosophy has never had the strength to make them one.

The tragic poet never insists on a solution, a supreme explanation, as the philosopher does. Is he wiser?

The straightest road to power is to declare misfortune cowardice, to shut one's eyes to sorrow, to the right of the meek, the gentle, and sick to exist. Pride, greed for power, desire for fame constantly shout: deny these!

But there is no authority other than human nature in its entirety, which consists for the most part of weakness, uncertainty, and longing for peace.

p.96, last par. To write something real is to live through it. People believe, the writer more so than anyone, that to live a book means to experience happenings and situations, which are rare, violent, grandiose. But that's not the way things are. To the contrary such "rare" and "grand" events generally make us neglect to think, to live deeply. Important events happen between the door and the street, between your four walls. The finest experiences in the world, those most moving and worthy of thought, are the ones we call slight and commonplace. Whoever faces such trifling occurrences thoughtfully achieves greatness. And, take note, he also encounters the most difficult thing of all. Make the attempt for one day only to be just, magnanimous, self-denying in confrontation with the everyday, and you will see that you stand face to face with—the heroic. Unless you gain your victory there, those rare and spectacular events won't bring you one step closer to truth and life.

p.117,#5 Pure or impure: if you settle for that, you'll get nowhere. Immaculate interest in truth is not for a human. Polarity is in everything. Without impurity no purity, no flame. To torture oneself with the question if one's quest is perfect or imperfect is as hopeless as wanting to determine if life is good or evil.

But on certain days I saw a span of the horizon over the sea, which to me was the embodied promise of the victory of human thought, and all that my heart held of Tantalus' blood seemed to call out: "Bring into your soul, bring with you in there the force of that span!"

Books.

Books that you finish with are not books at all. A true book is inex- p.119 haustible, like a truly lyrical poem. The real practitioners of the noble art of writing are recognizable because they offer the greatest pleasure on rereading. They are therefore of value only to those who know how to read—a species almost as rare as good authors.

The thin air of publicity! When a poet has become officially acknowledged and publicly hated, he is like a tree that has been moved from its good, protected place of growth in the woods out on the pavement of a city street. Modern literature is often pictured as a park or a garden. That jars one's mind.

Swedish.

There is a stream of light in Swedish! Light of April and flying skies. p.123,par1 We forget it, but all of what is best in us has that tinge. What is the sum of that which lives in the works of Tegnér;[1] if not the dream of this, the regret that life had become burlap instead of Swedish silk— Tegnér's real nature. Why not decide for the days of silk, for the light of April, for the fragrance of violets? Why was there only a wailing sound, the melancholy of an old man at the sight of youth? Spring is eternal in man, and one does not declare spring an intermezzo without being punished. There is arrogance in lamenting, which revenges itself. The poet plays with the dark, secretly convinced that the day is there beneath everything, and emerging. But in the end darkness must prevail in his work.

The scent of the Swedish language: violets in March. p.123,par2
The style of the Swedish language: I visualize the sea, blue on an April morning through a row of hazels in bloom.

The letter.

The best works by the finest writers have an illiterate touch. When an p.125 author has arrived at the stage where he clearly knows and can decide for himself what in him produces the unfading words, his real power is often gone. The scent has fled, he is plainly the literary worker. Faced with the thought of death, some regain the noble

[1]Famed 19th century Swedish poet.

spontaneity in old age. As did Thomas Carlyle. He then despised all that was labeled literature, and only wrote his Shakespearean letters—as I think they may be judged.

It is a shame that in our days letter writing, probably because of the increasing profiteering by means of the pen, has become a rarity. To be able to write letters that can endure scrutinizing in broad daylight one must have a relationship of innocence with the pen that is uncommon in "men of letters." A state of innocence that on the whole is the most essential ingredient of good style. "The best writers were those who were ashamed of being writers," says Nietzsche . . . There are also authors who really haven't written anything worth reading but their letters. And that's no minor feat.

The true letter is one of the greatest literary forms, precisely because it is not literary. Many women who hardly knew their syntax have written masterful letters—as long as they were in love.

One says that after *Frederick the Great*, Carlyle didn't write a major work. But how productive, how truly poetic, humanely beautiful, and magnanimous many of his letters to his friends from this period are (most of them to his sister and his two brothers, one of them in America). Was Carlyle ever great? Yes, he is here, in his eighties, walking in the day of fall through the old Scottish churchyard (Annandale), where his beloved ones rest: so silent and quiet now; those who in times past had such kind faces when they saw him approaching.

How trifling a human life, even when lived deeply and strongly and with hope by a "wise" man! And how often did he himself—one of the last of "the great readers"—make that reflection, when he turned the last page of such a book . . . "But an essay is no letter," says James Russell Lowell once in a letter, when he thinks he hasn't been pleasing enough. But sure, it is certainly a letter! As well as all that we write that is real and alive; letters to our friends, contemporary and future ones. Yes, Petrarch wrote letters to the dead as well! Isn't the whole human "culture" precisely that: an exchange of letters? We sit and read each other's letters, we acknowledge due receipt, and try to answer and express gratitude according to means.

Childhood.

p.127,par1 The earliest childhood memories are like faint flashes of lightning on the horizon of summer nights. They are frequently associated with particular sensations of taste and smell, impossible to capture, fluttering past like shadows when you try to catch them and look them square in the face. They might surface in moments of spiritual clarity and delight; as though electrically surging through one's whole system, you remember with the whole body, as it were; standing there before a darkness that seems charged with light, explosive, powerful. Moments that in their wake leave the purest joy, a feeling of immortality, a divination that says: nothing can be taken from you. The preexistence of the soul, as perceived in ancient philosophy, seems to be foreboded by this elation of memory, which hardly is equaled by anything in the life of the spirit.

Illness and misery our reprovers? But do they really show us what is right? Perhaps it would be asking too much to expect that they show us anything but that we are far from right, that we are captured by the wrong; and one has to be grateful for that. How many times would Epicurus have had to spit in his own face for saying that no fate can defeat the wise man? But yes, rest assured that even "the wise man" has to live through days and nights, when every drop of vitality is slowly tortured out of his body and he simply has to wait just like we other simple beings, wait until the sun graciously rises. p.139,#6

He who stands in the middle of the river of his enthusiasm finds it easy to talk with contempt about doubt and emptiness. But emptiness is a reality, and when it is there, nothing helps—let it rain.

But is it worth while?

Ignore! Ignore! That is for sure the height of all wisdom. And above all ignore your own shabbiness.

There are thoughts well worth living for, but don't get the idea that you are insured against all misery, which is still just as real! Definitely more so, according to some opinions, for those who have the strength to also feel the opposite side of things without permitting themselves to be crushed by the fact that there are those who look as though misery never touched them. They also suffered. p.139,#7

Everything beautiful wants to tell you something. Everything beautiful wants to become thought. p.140,#8 p.140,#11 One cannot believe in those who have no respect for joy and who lack the sacred sense of it. The whole of our human nature in its finest feeling revolts against the thought that the good and the joyful are just something negative, whereas the other (the misery) would be the essential and positive, the core of life. All you have to do to grasp this fact is to look into the eye of a small child.

p.141,#12 Suffering from "the injustices of the world" proves firstly that the one who suffers has plenty of time at his disposal. Those who really have been engaged in something important have been unaware of such things. They don't have the time.

p.142,#18 A thought is always something inexhaustible. There are no new thoughts. Originality discovers and reveals the significance of human thought.

p.145,#24 It makes me happy, when I hear the eighty-year-old Carlyle's remark on reading Plutarch: the difference between good and bad books is literally **immeasurable**.

Reading may only be a substitute for something better, but it is certainly no small thing to keep one's eyes open to the fact that some books are real books, a fact that few people have any feeling for.

Read these books often. They can only be read slowly. Books that you can read fast . . . ! You know a **book** among other things from the fact that it has to be read slowly. That there are people who can read it "fast" is not the fault of the book!

To read fast is as bad as to eat in a hurry.

I wish it were possible to express clearly what makes a book a real book.

Some believe the secret lies in something called "composition" for which they have an enormous respect.

Composition in a book; to use this most simpleminded of all stupid expressions—is equivalent to what the English call gentlemanliness: the gentle Shakespeare for example. It is the power of relating to the **human concern**, the love of it; it is the aroma of spring, clean, uncorrupted by worldliness, and free of convention.

The roar from a big city can sometimes be melodic, beneficial. Once I p.149,#29 had a room situated in such a way that the endless noise from the outside world, at some distance across a courtyard, assumed the likeness of a waterfall, of a mill in a creek, as caught by my ear on a quiet summer night. It absorbed and fused in its mass all individual torment and irritation.

To ask at once for the whole thing cut and dried is a great error. It p.149,#30 makes no sense to sit and wait for clarity, believing that your work will suddenly stand before you revealing in a flash the roads that led to it, free of charge. You have to grope your way in good faith and be content with little. In that way you keep your strength and courage alive. One frequently meets a very talented artist or poet lacking the capability of such slow, sinewy search, unwilling to put his hand to his work until he has got it as a kind of gift, and in some mysterious manner—of which he has a very unclear conception—with all difficulties and doubts blown away. Meanwhile, however, the strength seeps out of him simply because of lack of exercise, as a muscle languishes when it lies unused. And people with less talent but with more contentment surpass him easily. Whoever believes himself wise and "an instant genius" has closed all windows and doors to the truth, but whoever is aware of his weakness has opened them and will be rewarded.

Everywhere life is somberly, strongly Shakespearean. The distance p.150,#31 from any point to the holiest is equal.

To quote is dangerous. There are words so powerful, so blazing with p.151,#35 life that they burn right through a book, blot it out.

How do you recognize a good book? Among other things by feeling p.152,#37 and participating in the writer's joy of work. Real dullness lies, quite rightly, in the lack of joy. Because the inner nature of the spirit is joy.

When you have moved far away from yourself, when life has thrown p.153,#41 its huge rocks through your cobwebs, then contentment is a must. The road back home is long and difficult—one feels like despairing.

p.155,#43   In order to understand, one has to get completely lost in the thicket . . . Bad examples are of no use; you have to be on the brink of becoming one yourself before you will see clearly.

p.156,#47   Is there any will of thought without will to power? Yes, one of indescribable sweetness—when you are close to death.
Is this in your best interest?

p.156,#49   To read a "good essayist" is something terribly sad—as melancholy as witnessing an auction of old streetcar horses.

p.157,#54   Having lost all ambition, you succumb: unless in your mind's eye you discover at the same time the greatest and most divine of them all—to have none.

p.158,#57   The homelessness in life: you can carry it in your heart as a paralyzing, destructive power; and you can wear it as thunder and lightning around your head. It would be a loss, it would be the murder of your soul to close all doors to grief; but your grief is not the right sorrow unless it uplifts.

p.159,#60   There are passages in the works of some authors that in a way lie outside the frame of their writing, passages where you suddenly feel the man talking is not the literary worker So and So, but the human being, high above all "literature," clear, deep, good—but also with a wild tone, flying through the soul like the scream of a bird above a desolate ocean bay.

p.160,#64   Nothing is good enough for the sterile ones ("die Besserwisser").[1] Neither is anything good enough for the enthusiast. But that is a different matter!

p.160,#65   When you have arrived at the point where the most comfortable and interesting way seems to be to let the misery of life just go on irritating you, you swear at the futility of everything. But actually there is

[1]Know-it-all

only one comfortable and interesting way: not to let things irritate you. The world is not ugly; it is terrible, yes—but that is something entirely different.

Fostering the values of truth and beauty quiets the passions. But it p.169,#86 places us in a relationship to our fellow man that again stimulates passion. That the creative urge carries a profound erotic element in it, is noted by Plato, among others. It may seem strange that so few authors have been ambitious in a great and subtle sense; that the strategist of the word is such a rare phenomenon in our world. How easily one settles for utter futility, how easily one is satisfied! When you have secured a few thousand readers (buyers), regardless of what kind, you just keep the ball rolling year after year, content with maintaining a certain level without major effort. Just like most university professors when they have achieved tenure and can lay off their scientific work. Still, there are plenty of fine brains and fine hearts in the world, and there is nothing more stimulating in life, no sweeter incitement for the human need for power than the hope of becoming a living principle in the souls of profoundly living men. And what would be impossible for a true strategist of the word! The secret of great style is probably that it has been nourished by a refined desire for power, yes, surely you get at the heart of the matter if you make the oldest of all gods the prodigy of style . . . Eros.

Metron / 1918

---

p.25,#19 There is a feeling of joy and wisdom in hesitation which is far from the misery of indecision:
Cur non sub alta vel platano vel . . .[1]
The innermost grace in Montaigne.
Like a February day in the north, noon, warm sunshine on spruce, birch, and red tile roof—
There is a joy in this which surpasses every other, the "peaceable fruit of righteousness" (Hebr. 12:11) the joy of weighing darkness and light, anguish and clarity, having made one's soul into a balance of highest sensitivity.

p.27,#22 There is a road from contempt to—sun, for the very few. For a majority the road leads to barrenness and impoverishment. Great tolerance does not come from love.

p.28,#23 How hate and wrath can be made productive can be learned from the great workers who are belligerent and angry men. And here the teachers abound. But how sun, inspiration, and justice can grow in spite of the shadows of the demons, you won't learn from them; only from the very few, and they have quite a different pace.

p.30,#29 The loftiest sky is within your soul; the purest clarity is needed when you have to stand up against the mob within yourself. (There is a mob in every human being, just as there is one in every city, says Pro-

[1]Why not (rest) underneath the tall platan or . . . (Horace).

clus).[1] And that mob will never find a cleverer disguise than the foolish agony caused by "the world's injustices," your humiliations and rejections.

Wanting to needle, hurt, annoy—that's the inspiration of the know-it-all. p.31,#30

In the British you seldom find a certain enthusiastic *candidezza* (candor) in the mood and pathos of life. "Good sense" always seems to be the quality they praise the most. Their relation to antiquity does not have the fire of a Montesquieu or a Winckelmann (Montaigne on the other hand could very well have been an Englishman). Even in antiquity their intent was "good sense." Seldom clearly distinguishable in the English character is the fine line of joy that runs through the great French era, on the borderline of which the maturing Goethe stands, and that breathed such a fine, good breeze into his spirit. What was Johnson's "constitutional melancholy" but an insensitivity to this candid element, the Hellenic, the French classical, the Lessing-Goethe light. Carlyle struggled vehemently to maintain himself in this element, but then it definitely did not mix with violent fervor. As in most other men of genius, the most productive quality in Johnson and Carlyle is their capacity to confess uncertainty, unworthiness, suffering, and weakness. p.32,#33

The only thing worth obtaining is what you get for free: by virtue of having the right ear, the right discipline—the quiet, mild, and forceful discipline—which gets its strength from mildness, its mildness from strength. The pushy climber never knew that force. p.33,#34

> *Ja, das ist das rechte Gleis,*
> *Wenn man nicht weiss,*
> *was man denkt;*
> *Alles ist als wie geschenkt.*[2]

For free, yes! But how much patience, how much ardent watchfulness against all that is crude, all that jars and squeaks, and that does not have the good tone in feeling and thought, have necessarily been endured before a human being reaches this state!

[1] Greek philosopher, 411?–485.
[2] "Yes, that is being on the right track. When one does not know what one thinks, when one thinks; All is as though it were a gift" (Goethe).

p.35,#36 A strong, beautiful, wise, and happy person, strong and beautiful even in misfortune, was always something so rare and foreign that you may imagine the myth of Apollo, a persistent legend about an exceptional individual, created from a historical truth. On some occasion every artistic and philosophical man experiences in himself this vision: the god. He experiences it in desperation's bliss, when all his power rises and wants to hold on to the light of this image with a hundred arms, drink it with his being's every drop of blood. Just as every genuine child feels the sun shine right into his chest in quite another way than grownups do; at their peak those strong, tall children, the Greeks, had the strength to feel the sun of beauty's goodness kalokagathia[1] burn Eros with a strange sweetness into their blood—a generosity and a spring splendor in man's spirit which we cannot even guess at with our pushiness, our competition gone sour. No wonder that the god was a reality to these people, when the fire of divinity shone over life.

p.36,#37 If you look at life with its unlimited crudeness, ugliness, overindulgence, confusion, and distortion, then art, moderation, philosophical joy, and composure appear as the most absurd and adventurous of all luxuries; and one has to smile at those who are amazed at a materialistic philosopher who believes in gods. Such people have never really sensed that art and philosophy are divine things. Emptyheaded and with empty hearts they only babble about it. Hence their amazement at Epicurus.

The more one reaches the depths of the Hellenic soul, the clearer it becomes how weak, lax, and spiritless our whole concept of beauty and wisdom is.

p.55,#63 The more you find your strength heightened by forgiving, the more inclined you become to forgive.

To become pure at heart through egoism? If this could be the case . . . is the view less beautiful because the road leading up to it is slippery?

p.58,#69 There are kinds of men who are a blend of savagery and weakness; the foundation of their souls resembles the dark, brushy, rock-in-

[1]Goodness of beauty.

fested ground where April's bright blue and yellow flowers shimmer. They rarely reach the height and sweetness of summer, but the scent of earth, water, and early flowers in the coarse April air around them is sometimes just as indestructible as that of ripeness.

If you despair of the power of your thought to render happiness, then p.60,#72 blame your disbelief, your timidity, and carelessness. Thought rarely abandons the cautious. It is in its nature to be offended by all exaggerations. It will put up with restrained remorse, but will shun crude, excessive lamentation.

Everyone needs some form of narcotic—because that is the way of p.61,#75 life! It is with what one drugs one's self that makes a difference.
    Is virtue itself not a form of narcotic! What is "culture?" *Quid pure tranquillet.*[1]

"Optimism," and buckets of it nowadays! One could use it for hog- p.61,#77 feed . . . And one does! Or did the world ever see swine looking so smooth, shiny, and optimistic as today?

Who can afford to do without ambition? It seems there were a few p.62,#78 who did. But you will soon find that their own ambition made them despise ambition. So much thirst groans in the lines of Nietzsche:
        Diese Münze, mit der alle Welt bezahlt:
        Ruhm!
        Nur mit Handschuhen fasse ich sie . . .[2]
    Yes, that really seems to be the whole difference: with or without gloves. It is hardly worth mentioning.

There is a kind of noble curiosity. Who understood the art of put- p.62,#79 ting his ear to the books like Montaigne!

[1]Truly calming (Horace).
[2]These coins with which the whole world pays
 Glory!
 Only with gloves on will I touch them . . .

p.63,#80 The author must believe there are people who need him; need him as he needs himself and his innermost core in the days and times when he is deserted by his powers and can hardly grasp how they once belonged to him.

p.63,#81 Sorrow is nearer to light than wrath. In ire you are completely shut out, you are not even capable of longing for purity.

p.64,#87 The day is like a stranger of divine origin, wishing to pay you his visit. You're fortunate, if he finds you at home.

p.65,#88 The more you realize that to live is the highest art, the greater the hope that you will cherish life.

p.65,#89 The most characteristic feature of modern spiritual debasement is the deep respect shown for the needling, the leering, the skeptically sour-sweet, the superciliously ironic and whatever it may be called—all this petty spiritual squalor that passes for intelligence. Where is the grand free tone, the bright noble glance? Impertinence! Long live impertinence! It alone is gentlemanlike in the modern culture of hucksters. What an insult to French culture when such is called Gallic! All *dédain* and impertinence is foreign to the great Frenchmen—they are true Lycians and Atticans. Montaigne, Vauvenargues, Montesquieu, La Rochefoucauld: theirs is the great spiritual French style; spiritual, yes—like the Acanthus stems on a Corinthian capital.

p.67,#92 Why do away with your ambitions? For the sake of your well-being? To stroll about in contentment? No, to make room inside you; room for the only ambition you can live on, the one of truth.

p.67,#94 How shall we gain freedom? By finding something for which it is worthwhile to sacrifice one's mob instincts and tendencies for weakness. What one loves, one becomes.

p.68,#95 What a waste of time, strength, and eyesight, when one prefers to look out through a dim, soiled windowpane, when next to it is a clean and clear one! Only read books of great style: thus you keep your soul and your eyes healthy.

Those who speak with disdain about philosophy and life as being p.68,#97
impossible in secluded rooms, know nothing about the meaning of
adventure.

There are situations in life when you cannot keep what you hold p.69,#98
most dear except by forsaking it. Then watch out for the "heart!" It
talks sweetly—until it has lured you into a trap. Then it leaves you
and you no longer have even your sorrow. From sorrow it is not far to
joy. But from wrath and hate deserts extend, impenetrable scrub-
wood of thorn. You have to make a choice and that may be terribly
difficult; for the heart is as strong as reason, and you must fall on your
knees and beg for mercy, pray to something above—genius, guardian angel, lodestar . . . Then you will know what prayer is, about
which the stupid ones laugh.

There may be a conflict between truth and ambition, and there can p.71,#103
be boldness in gentleness. That is something youth cannot comprehend.

Reading many books causes you to grow slight, reading a few makes p.72,#105
your spirit full-blooded. The fact that it is so easy to get hold of books
nowadays has ruined many a heavy lightweight. It never ruins the
strong, for they always know how to escape to the fresh wells, the secluded meadows surrounding the wellsprings, deep inside the silence of the woods. The names of these springs are on everyone's lips,
but few know the trails leading to them. How shall you find your
way? How did Odysseus get to speak to the shadows? Give them
blood—if you have any. From every corner of the world the busy-
bodies came running to Goethe with oceans of—ink. But did he respond? We haven't heard.

Hatred among authors—he who has the best public is always the p.73,#107
most vehemently hated. Authors hate each other not so much for the
superficial and more obvious success. And that is certainly a very
good sign.

When we want to describe one of the purest forms of happiness, p.77,#113
we—the modern ones—call it "productive joy." But we then really

mean a passionate state of mind, in which hope and expectation make up the main elements. These elements are crude and pathological to the philosopher of antiquity. His desire lies on a much higher level. Greek psychology is the psychology of desire. It is vital to grasp how the Epicurean god determines real states of the soul and values of life, to realize that he is far from being a romantic dream product: when you get this far, you have come close to the soul of antiquity, its religion, its thought of redemption. Unique in the history of culture is the curiosity of the Greek philosopher's persona: the urge to track down the highest possibilities and arts of desire.

p.78,#114 *Metron* does not necessarily exclude excessiveness in the common (bourgeois) sense. But what it always and everywhere excludes by necessity is—mediocrity.

This is also the case with love and truth. Someone who never let a lie pass his lips, may be of a thoroughly deceitful nature, foreign to all *veracitas*. And a frivolous liar may be *verax* with all his heart.

p.84,#121 A poet should never write when his mind is in a tumult of passions. This may one day become obvious, like the fact that one should never sit down to a meal with dirty hands.

Yet, it is said, no one has ever become an artist or a philosopher without great passions.

Rubbish!

It is precisely for this reason we have an interest in art and culture at all. The road leading up to the temple is precipitous, but the temple does not reel.

Whoever rightly appreciates the fullness of sunshine and joy, also loves a certain coolheaded moderation and modesty, for they belong together. What little one really finds out about life, one only learns by virtue of those two . . .

p.101, #128 The thought that your ideal will not be of any help to you when life tears into your heart's core, should not deter you from an unceasing, ardent attention to that ideal. Perhaps there will come a time when it seems nonsensical to you to attempt to understand the difference between the measured and measureless, between composure and excessiveness, *charis* and barbarism, order and disintegration—moments when everything proves insufficient: that may well be. But the ideal was a reality in a few men's lives; *ataraxia* (calmness of mind), measure, and *charis* stood out as preservers of order, love of light and life, sufficient protection against the most violent blows dealt by fate. This was reality in the lives of a few of the greatest men. Should one avoid the joy of observing this ideal; its reality in the lives of these men, only because one harbors a well-founded fear of confronting a day when the weight of this ideal will crush you?

Perhaps a certain childlike conscious-unconscious hypocrisy existed in all culture enthusiasm and all talk about liberation through striving for truth and beauty.

In fear we know that deep in the darkest corner of our hearts demons sit laughing at us and at our educational pranks. In all clear and good people this outlook, this consciousness, becomes the source of the beautiful golden-pure humor, the all-forgiving, all-understanding smile, which is the hallmark of really superior thought. And what was the eventual reward for all this, life's whole, great, meager gain? Surely, nothing more, nothing greater than what Horace points at in the most low-keyed, golden-pure words he has written:

> *et amara lento*
> *temperet risu.*[1]

[1] . . . and may ease the bitterness / with a gentle smile.

Selected Writings and Essays (Poetry, Criticism, Life and Truth) / 1920

p.146,#4 The critic, the psychologist of culture, must to a certain extent have the eye of a botanist, have a secretly developed, special sense for the locale of rare plants.

This is especially true of the moralist, and in particular of one who dedicates himself to moral speculation regarding the human possibilities of happiness. He has to have the highly developed senses of an American Indian, an unerring nose for tracking down the lightest steps of any deity—those of happiness. Yes, there are spots in the woods of history and human culture where this god touched the ground and breathed unfading fragrance over matter; places walked by the unknowing, but with exhilarated bliss by those who know.

p.148,#8 When we learn how we are changed by the years and by our experiences, how what seemed like the highest wisdom at one stage turns to empty wind at the next juncture—we feel tempted to think that it would be nonsense to ever strive for an integral vision of the life and the situation of a human. Still, there are many grades in this school! And this school is not of the kind where any guarantees are given for what is being served. There are classes even for what is false and twisted, and even those things can be useful to the life-diet. Maybe you learned to see sharper and farther by mistake and faulty calculation than you would otherwise have done.

There is a craving for knowledge; there are diseases, infections that are useful. In order to do justice to what is sound, it sometimes doesn't hurt that soundness has something to wreak its vengeance on, and with real enthusiasm.

Those who have seen profoundly through the ages have not been those best versed in history. They have had the sense to ask for directions on their way, and therein lay their productive power. p.151,#12

Selected Writings and Essays (Equinox) / 1922

p.165 Equinox! It should always be equinox. And light is ever new. It is the gray, worn, and rough demonic scab of Every day that doesn't let it through. Every day should be like a journey in a miraculous land, where nobody has ever walked. Presumptuousness! one says. But those who strive to invite the day home with them speak in a different manner. We complain of how life debases us and that all is a conspiracy to ruin our finest faculties—so we fold our arms and act highbrow!

All hesitation should cease, all doubts be dispersed by these words of Plato: "Neither the day nor the night suffice for those who are anxious to use their reason." Every situation should be subordinated to this statement; your entire relationship to existence and your environment are ruled and explained by it.

On the Ocean Shore / 1922

p.86

Don't look back with disdain upon the contempt, fear, and bitterness of youth! It had the confident divination of home and of security; there was the good instinct of a precious joy and safety on the other side of the world of Vulgus; there was thought's tender consciousness, will to sacrifice and self-denial among all the recklessness, rashness, and contempt. There was the divination that the love of the unattainable is the only thing great and solid in life.

Don't speak so superciliously of this rebelliousness, this self-torture, this love of pain. There have been and are those, whom contemptuousness eventually taught to love other, more refined and precious pains, more refined and precious rebellions: who were taught the courage to take on the painful cure of having the sicknesses of their souls, their injustice, and their untruthfulness burnt out of their secret hidings.

Dependence.p.88

Under your own yoke or that of a stranger: take your choice!

The starving.p.88

The starving understand each other. Who understood the dark gaze in Nero's eye better than—Kierkegaard!

p.88 Difficulty—impossibility.

It is hard to live a true life. Still not as hard as to live a true life—halfway. Because that is impossible. But it is this impossibility that makes us suffer—not the difficulty mentioned previously.

p.89 Feeling.

For art, for learning: through the highest degree of refinement of feeling. Shouldn't that lead to the true, most elevated intellectuality!

Those wise ones: each drew a line of shrewdness through his soul; with the cunning of inexhaustible vigil he transformed it into a line of clarity, love, and gentleness. "Be cautious as snakes and innocent as doves." Truly, the cause of culture, refinement, and the love of truth has never been more clearly expressed.

p.90 To enter a blossoming forest.

To enter the woods where the flowers blossom in spring creates the same feeling as if entering a world of spirits, as if silence enters—as though talking, singing voices suddenly lower themselves to whispers of secrecy. Who knows what is said in the woods when nobody is there!

p.92 Light.

The light puts out all pain. Light is the coolest of all.

p.93 The brevity of life.

Is there anything more gorgeous than the white, Nordic sky of June! How many June mornings are there in a human life? They are not hard to count—and least of all those that one really encountered!

p.93 Pride.

If you want to keep your head high: fall on your knees. Man is human only in reverence.

p.94 Trees.

How trees know how to mourn! The dryad in the city's wilderness of brick and mortar, between the sparkle of streetcar cables and the roar of cars, is not the same peaceful creature as in the woods or countryside. Ovid would have depicted the spirits of criminals as condemned to languish in these crowns wilting at the height of summer, and the poets of the Greek anthology would have made them whine in impressionistic epigrams. Trees are creatures that thrive among good people; the crowd looks down upon them and finds it ridiculous to enjoy such things. Trees may well be the happiest and most beautiful beings of the creation, and evoke strong feelings when they are humiliated and outraged. A tree speaks to you of superior piety and bliss; your mind is refreshed and soothed when approaching its genius, looking at it with your inner vision. How many trees were guardian spirits, and teachers for the children who grew up under their protection and never forgot the whisper of their branches.

It is much easier to deny yourself something entirely than partially. p.232 The former provokes, concentrates, and keeps you excited; but as soon as you give in—even slightly—you have corrupted it all.

There is a muscle in your soul which will forever languish, unless you p.232 maintain your hunger—hunger in every sense of the word. And life depends on this muscle.

Wherein lies our lack of freedom? In not daring to reach for freedom. p.242
    We sit like children with the movement of a precious timepiece in our hands: take it to pieces—pieces of learning.

To act presumptuous won't do—but it may well pay to stretch your p.241 thoughts beyond the toes you are going to turn up one day in the four planks of a wooden box.

In regretting one has to be grateful to one's repentance. That is the p.241 way to ignore one's regrets.

Nothing is rarer than the clear face! But nothing is more common p.241 than the effort to show such a face to the world: the clear face strained by affectation.
    What ruins the clarity is so very often—the sagacity.

p.238 Real admiration is a moral force that can lead to liberation. The more real your devotion becomes, the more space will be created within you. Poverty: lack of room. For many admiration is a kind of exorcism.

p.233 Freedom is the ability to ignore what you cannot change. Then life flows toward you out of the smallest and the simplest things, and suddenly you have your hands full.

Letting be what you cannot change! If one could learn that art, one would be free at once. And thus, precisely the change would have taken place!

Selected Writings and Essays (Menandrean World) / 1922

Evenness in the Greek sense is a tableland, evenness in a modern p.186 sense—is rarely more than flatness.

The Danes who talk so much about their (weakness) evenness, could have learned something about it from—Kierkegaard. He knew this tableland, he had been there, but he did not want to stay there, nor could he. To flatness he had no way of coming; —so he stepped (overstepped) up to a human-unhuman, where you can neither nest nor live. But flatness would please him least of anything! Because flatness is always sub human. The unnatural in Kierkegaard has its origin in a noble nature.

Evenness, the softest of all, ties down all demons. To fetter lastingly what is most dangerous and dark, only the softest and brightest is of any use.

That innermost sustaining, protective power within all those who p.190 never could be satisfied—an absurd expectation safeguarded in darkness, secluded, defended in faithfulness, nourished and supported by the soul's finest juices. What is its name? . . .

All greatest poetry flows together with this. And what would poetry deal with, if not the superhuman expectation, the sweet absurdity, the possible—impossible.

Nothing proved strong and secure enough for them but—the most fragile, the hardest to tie down. They found a foothold only on the most evasive ground. Evasive—but an elusiveness packed with enchanting absurdities! They had learned that it was always worth their while to mark with secret signs and tokens for their inner vision the most beautiful, when they happened to catch a glimpse of it, to try then again and again to trace their steps back and proceed farther into the light-mixed dark. There is a cunningness and a method of knowledge in this life of love, in this hypersensitivity to light. Mysticism! one says. But all sublime will and urge for beauty is mysticism.

p.194 Emotional control is a productive state of mind, a favorable breeze for the sail of the spirit.

Breeze, yes! There were a few who wagered all their love on precisely the finest wind, the most beautiful weather. They understood the art of outwitting their sentiments, to play with them—but playing with them as though in earnest. It is this beautiful game that is also called—art . . .

p.200 In the problem, the freedom-problem, lies our only freedom.

No wonder that philosophy exercises such magic on the human mind! Philosophy that holds for us the prospect of capturing the superhuman: the calm . . .

p.201 How few—those who understood what kind of prey happiness is! Still they were not so few that their pursuit has not drawn a line throughout the human experience that can never die, which will always attract followers. The life of a human was often likened to the seasons; and there is something to that. Spring you get for free, and very often it does not turn out too well. The bad weather and the cold are also for free, whichever way you turn. But one of the seasons is not presented to you as a gift: summer! You have to create it yourself with the joint efforts of noble powers. Everything conspires to stifle within us the possibility of sweetness and ripeness. Sourness was taken seriously by everybody; the sour and the unripe became the very acme, and the clarity and ripeness—an intermezzo. That this is the summit of life was understood and retained by very few.

Western–Eastern / 1925

It would be a great misfortune if the fine art of understanding pov- p.205
erty, understanding living with simplicity, lightness, and solidarity,
should become rare, if life should let itself be overcome by contriv-
ance.

The great enthusiasts of the spirit are foulmouthed like Luther, and p.266
not afraid of descending to places where others, the delicately soulful
ones, have to hold their noses. On the contrary, they seem to receive
great inspiration from such places; it is as though the predicament of
man moved their senses right there, where the faith in man's dignity,
his pride, appear threatened. Did they ever forget, did they ever try to
cover up or lie away the ugliness, the horror of life! They descended
to the cave of Trophonios[1], but—with the honeycomb.

It seems obvious to me that the solution, what we call "truth," is only p.268
to be found in the personality, in the character, and in the custody
of it. Thus, I can, to a certain extent, reconcile myself with the contradictions in the great personalities. Above all I see Goethe. The same
and perhaps even more so, seems to apply to a man who stands out as
a Goethe of the Orient—Sadi.
  It seems to me as though the essence of their wisdom was to be
found largely in a forcefully guarded professional secret. "Ear-

[1]Greek architect, builder of the temple of Delphi.

nestness!" they say. But we know a thing or two about what human seriousness really is! It is more, and also less, than what the word says. That's why we "fable," and call it truth. Don't despair of the contradictions. But note well this: that we stick to, believe in our personality. This is our truth. Hasten to do the same, and you will find: East and West: Man—Man? The question mark, we call man.

Between Passions / 1927

Murmur of woods, birdsong, and silence—that is our spirit breath- p.47,#69
ing, our solitude and our oneness with life, oneness of art and nature.
Those who are bound by this freedom, and those who bind by means
of this freedom, they are the ones who have drawn the soothing and
pure and great line in our culture; they dwell on the unbroken
ground of a joy that is fit to rule in art—work of art called Life, work
of art called Culture.

Yes, wherein lies that which is fundamentally worth calling crea- p.37,#51
tive in any spiritual work, except in the power to direct that which—
at any given moment of life—feels the ray of a certain star brush past
the face, making it turn toward the region of this light with deep re-
solve.

The ability to give protection and form to things that belong to the p.48,#72
most vulnerable of our inner world, things in the sign of holy
aidos[1]—is certainly worthy of our gratitude. The real treasure hunt-
ers in the human spirit harbored a living love of form: a love that
sprang from reverence. The loose and tattered, the disorderly vibrat-
ing, frequently rests on the same ground of a defective sense of reverence as that which is lifelessly dignified, dully shining, and ele-
gantly "perfect in form" . . .

[1]Reverence.

p.50,#77 The most precious quality we possess has a tinge of the sky's blue and the lark's song—and if we could apply that color and that tone to thought and life . . . In the Swedish "timidity" lies a great sane and fertile principle—an *enkráteia* (restraint) of the heart, which in the final analysis is still the best bulwark to provide faith and creative strength.

p.56,#87 There is only one path that leads to a life of seclusion and its happiness. But that is a King's highway—authenticity. On that road you truly don't run the risk of being noticed.

p.62,#101 To believe in something achieved, a success, a "victory"—that is like throwing one's most precious valuables out the window.

To have a good scornful laugh at one's self—hard, without mercy, into the most secret and sore hiding places of one's character and nature—that is most necessary and indispensable for whoever loves (the dream of . . .) clean hands.

p.71,#120 The solitude that does not defend and prove itself by communion is neither whole nor strong. This has been felt by those who are truly lonely. And if you want to find out where the words came from that have proved to be the most durable, the most inevitable, and filled with the most profound empathy, you shall find they are the words of people regarded as alien to life and reality while they were alive— who lived the reality that others chased in the empty clatter of society's clamor. They had no contempt for man. But they certainly feared the agony always lurking within, the agony and danger of feeling that contempt for man.

p.77,#130 The only way to make a human humble, unselfish, and consequently happy—make him into a god! That was the dream of antiquity's philosophy.

p.86,#148 In all productive life this is decisive: your relation to the world of wishes.

The same goes for flower bulbs! You must grow them slowly in cool rooms to get the most beautiful flowers. If you force them with too much heat they become puny.

Therefore, Frederick the Great was of the opinion that princes and men of genius share the ability to disregard their personal need for happiness. Thus they safeguard their own. And when Caesar awoke in the fat trap—the trap of Power—and saw that he must go on or succumb, it was already too late. "The light and lean ones" came upon him: those who had been on his side, his comrades according to nature.

It is precisely certain great men's weight that taught them their p.90,#153 greatest wisdom and finest stratagem: dignity, most of all before one's self!—reticence, fear of comfort *"sich gehen lassen!"*[1]—the weight that whispered in their ear the most joyful learning and discovery: that between dignity and lightness there exists a deep and secret relationship.

Is there a bad conscience in this? What is it in man that rises to the heights but bad conscience . . . a sick, an ugly, a poor conscience! Eros—*Penia*.[2] In this respect Christianity and Plato have said the same. One's good conscience one can do without.

The life of spirit and thought is only lived profoundly when one p.104, #178 knows and has one's heart set upon this: the impossibility of being someone who could or would assert himself in this world; only when he deeply and voluntarily wills his romantic *locus standi*, his beyond this world! In this lies the eternally Eastern mark of all devoted life possessing distinct character. This trait of aristocracy is decisively oriental and—human. It has always been acknowledged—as mystical empty talk—but seldom in a heartfelt way. For from culture one wants something else, something that stimulates the marketplace. But thus one has also achieved a beyond of an altogether different kind.

One leads one's own way. Dante molded his will into what he called p.106, #183 "Virgil" and "Beatrice," made visible its *daimon, genius, fylgia*[3] to the

[1]Take it easy.
[2]Poverty.
[3]Ancient Norse guardian angel.

eye of his nature. He leads his own way, he is the inner land's discovery, which he reached by being faithful to his own nature's possibilities.

p.111, #193 The great rule is always valid: against passion nothing will do but passion.

To become my own master, master myself—this I can only achieve by transforming myself into the passion by which I want to be governed. This way I slake my thirst for power; this is called control, self-restraint, desire for self-domination.

When one has learned to handle the weapon called passion, one has learned to live. Has one then also learned to be a human? This question is really the question of man.

p.115, #201 If you find the value of life in your ability to see things in a bright, sure, and calm light—then your outlook can never be dark enough. The good pessimism is the good, dark eye common to all men of light: the *ataraxi*[1] of watchfulness. By that glance such men are to be recognized.

He who wisely cares for his fear, also protects the need for his love of light. And true joy can only be attained through purest need and desire. The world is full of pessimistic rentiers.

p.117, #204 It can be said that man lives in a kind of marriage with himself—it is certainly tempting to term this a kind of *mésalliance*, but one should not be too sure on that point . . . The hard conditions of the human psyche depend upon this, and speaking so candidly of "feminism," one might do well to scrutinize this basic relationship. It is here the real struggle is carried on; our profound and beautiful—*duel domestique* . . .

p.117, #205 From the great ones you learn to have your doubts about them. But one does not cease to respect them. One sees the inevitable *quodlibet*[2] quality in everything human—even in all that we call genuine.

[1]Indifference.
[2]Whatever you like.

They too might have had their "family secrets." But at the point when they declare their own insolvency, you are by no means offered a lesser view.

p.117, #206

One has to be blinded, says Luther. If not, nothing will be accomplished. For if we clearly see what kind of people we are dealing with—how petty and filthy everything is—we would never care to lift a finger.

p.118, #207

I believe that all of them, the men of devotion and heroic courage, have seen the situation in this light, that they purposely let themselves be blinded in the interest of inspiration, deed, and the urge for accomplishment.

There is nothing beautiful in man. Yet we suffer terribly when we have sinned against anything fair. And maybe that is—fair enough.

p.118, #208

"Man is a swine," say the Germans. And that is true enough. It is fitting to be sensitive regarding this assumption, so that it then turns out to be good enough. But that which is more than good enough, is yet not fair enough.

p.119, #210

The zoological way of looking at man is a soothing way, an "antiphilogistic" way.

p.119, #211

It seems to me as though Swift best illustrates this situation—the repulsiveness of his tales.

Among religious men Luther offers the same kind of illustration. Luther and Swift may well be the "crudest" of all modern writers. Both men were filled with great passion contained in hearts of equal darkness.

There is a great wisdom in this. It kept them within the *bathos*[1] of their powers, collected their strength, held them together—by means of coolness.

This is the aspect of Greek philosophy worth seeing, worth—living.

Play the game: the road of life of the greatest men—if you look at its width—basically follows nothing but the common course of men,

p.120, #213

[1]Lowness.

the road of misery. Yes—it even becomes part of the greatness they achieved (that which has nothing to do with the width of the trail). It does not appeal to us to always keep in mind this self-evident fact. And that provides precisely the sublime effect of their work. For a few moments we glimpse something purely human, without restraint. They have played—gambled, gambled away everything.

p.122, #215   The confession-in-disguise of the inadequacy of all that he has lived and fought for, the sense of the hollowness of his fame, kneeling before his own innermost demands: that is the genuine and valuable I now find everywhere in the writings of Ibsen—every place where he is really honest and "great." The disguise is the real Ibsen, and it is remarkable that in a final analysis it is on the ground of this confession-in-disguise—only vaguely sensed by most people—that his great fame is founded. Ibsen possesses in his personality a mystique of the saga, which links him with the Orient!

p.122, #216   What was given, was given to him with severe conditions. He could not always submit to them: he went into hiding, defaulted—sometimes with the honest intent that he might succeed—that he might have the right to attempt to live under common, less difficult circumstances. Then—eventually—when he realized that the sophistry of his attempt at fleeing was nothing but wind and emptiness, bad conscience came upon him.

How poor a human life! And often it is hard to determine whether someone was impoverished by neglect, or by his zeal, whether poor by extravagance or by greed.

p.124, #219   Would it be possible to say that Henrik Ibsen might have been happier had less fortune come his way? Would he then have had to moan so dismally over the necessity to balance the scales—could this have turned into the nourishment of his strength and his daily bread as in the case of a St. Martin? Or take note here how a Solness-mystery expresses itself in him: "It is from my own experience I can say that the daily food for a human with spiritual needs is a small piece of the genuine cross soaked in the tears of a prophet. Woe to him if he lets a day pass without taking nourishment from this dish! Then he has not eaten his daily bread."

The background! The great fresh, the dark one—he knew how to keep it and stand by it. p.126, #221

"*Fossens gru og sange!*"[1]

The background! The dark, the fresh—the joyous, which gives strength; the sanctuary of value and dignity: he remained faithful to it, by it he succeeded in living his life, stature intact.

The way soul and art have joined in him makes him outstanding forever.

In the end he began to question and doubt the inner and outer isolation that was the prerequisite for his spiritual and artful existence, doubting its righteousness; suspecting it was an encroachment against life. One might say it was the Kierkegaard quality—always deep in his nature—that had now emerged. p.127, #222

The solitude of the devotedly living and the devotedly creative; the character of loneliness, highest culture's relation to life: here you may appreciate the great, dark Rousseau-theme that even in Ibsen is the central point; the theme which only classicism, the metrics-mystique the Greek soul has been capable of solving—"dissolving"—and yet . . .

In reading Ibsen—1867—Julius Lange was disturbed by an "overworked soul that ruins everything." This proves that Julius Lange knew what art is, but also that he did not know who Ibsen was. Well, that is easy for us to say! And after Solness, says Brandes, he recognized the greatness of Ibsen, yes, found him "awesomely great." p.127, #223

It is not only the suspicious attitude of the Nordic soul toward art that reveals itself in Ibsen; in this context he is representative. And thus by his true, great relationship to art he becomes still more Nordic; far more so than for example, Strindberg.

The power of magic he dreams of and wants—he wants it for the sake of mastery, a captivating power over life. p.129, #226

Thus he learns—and is his own victim, himself the prisoner. This is the ancient trait of song and saga. It seems profound and "tragic." But yet it does not reach the bottom; it is only the popular, the senti-

[1]The rapid's torment and song!

mental surface. It does not reach down to that which the Nordic seldom attains: art and perfection and captivity's freedom.

Thus even Ibsen is caught in the Nordic: a captive of his *koglende kvad*,[1] blaming the force into whose powers he has delivered himself.

p.129, #228 An author is not very efficient unless in his nature he has a certain *deinōtēs*[2]—something "demonic," secretly at work, perhaps something akin to the mesmeric influence exercised by certain great conquerors in the field.

Among Nordic men I found this trait to be—if strongest I don't know, but at least most clearly demonstrated—in Kierkegaard. And next in Ibsen.

If one is looking for a criterion to illustrate the classic concept *deinōtēs* in any of the great literary characters of modern times, Ibsen ought to be primarily considered.

p.130, #229 *Jeder ächte Künstler ist als einer anzusehen, der ein anerkanntes Heilige bewahren und mit Ernst und Bedacht fortpflanzen will.*[3]

Sometimes it is hard to avoid a certain feeling of sadness: when realizing that everything sensible has already, many times over, been excellently expressed—and expressed in vain. And note how well-hidden, pushed into obscurity, drowned by triviality's overwhelming mass—therefore, how important it is that the sensible be repeated again and again, experienced in new individuals over and over with new variations, with a new emphasis, in a new voice—continuously kept alive.

p.131, #231 Whose is the Word? Whose is the Thought? His who loves them. This is finally the possibility of Newness. For "saying that something is new" is nonsense.

p.131, #232 Only he who has **direction** is capable of **newness**. Others have—variations, news.

[1]Incantation.
[2]Fascinating power.
[3]Every real artist is to be considered as someone who will keep alive something acknowledged as holy and make it live on earnestly and thoughtfully (Goethe, 1811).

Newness is a matter of morality. Your productive criterion is precisely newness. p.131, #233

But to the world, being new is to be different, and that is the sin, if he loves newness, he most bitterly expiates.

How one acquires newness—might prove extremely decisive. p.133, #236

It is the way to deal with change (frequently confused with newness) that is the source of power that creates newness. The greater this power, the greater one's capacity to endure monotony: hence a noble monotony, the most precious one.

"Erase and go on." p.136, #242

Erasing by proceeding. Obliterate only by unswerving attitude and lasting action; never episodically. Then you dig in, deepen and obscure the track.

Life's feat: the eye's ongoing regeneration. The struggle is about newness.

This is the cold bath, life's winter adventure with a tone of the *Iliad—proi d'hypeoioi*[1]—to break up the ice under the red sky of dawn! Again and again.

Whoever has finally found his role—his nature—and learned to use it skillfully, has nothing to expect from this world. (Because the world does not want skill, but—brisk business!) He has "played his role." Thus he can also calmly be buried—if he is foolish enough to expect something from the world. p.136, #243

Rule creates adventure. p.136, #244

Under "rule" you penetrate the depths of life-romanticism. Someone rich does not make a lot of noise. He is in the hands of Rule, unswervingly, safeguarding free vision's capture, the power to create adventure. The secret of his riches? His dampening capacity.

For "the gray in life" is the brook, never drying up, ever flowing and—for the majority—in vain. But the magic flute of "Rule" played its tones into his ear. And he understood.

There is something childish in every genius, but in a different and

[1]Under the red sky of dawn.

greater sense than commonly understood. It lies in the fact that all in him is designed, created, and directed to safeguard the power that brings adventure.

In his sacred way of viewing the world freshly with a childish eye of romantic Newness, he is—a classic.

p.137, #245 Again and again something new reveals itself as soon as one takes an earnest step toward integrity; as soon as one tries to unchain the fetters of the despot—Selfishness; as soon as one tries to breathe in noble freedom's love. Life becomes decrepit only through selfishness. That is the reason life's newness is so difficult—and yet so divinely easy— to discover. And art and culture are within a hair's breadth of being as rare as goodness!

p.141, #253 What does antiquity teach us? Reverence, piety, just as when one ponders the sight of any pure, genuine, and common face, grown old from human experience, simple, hardy experience.

Such reverence and wondering humility is the foundation (resonance) of song, and art, and wisdom, the antidote for everything hybrid and all shallow pessimism. Nevertheless, this firm and whole foundation is very rarely encountered among the practitioners of song, art, and the art of thought.

p.141, #254 "The day is too short!" they said. Life's day too short!

The day was too big for them. The day is the armor and a sword that only self-control, the governor-servant, is capable of handling, and which only the responsible self can lift.

p.143, #256 The Great decision often finds its way through the markedly simple and colorless. Such constraint the Greeks called music.

When we look for the most decisively important things in life, we seem most anxious to turn our backs on this sphere of existence. But we cannot give enough thought to the Simple things! That is, by contemplating the fact that the first consideration for an explorer's expedition, a journey toward new land, irrevocably lies in leaving the old one.

And how is it possible to forget something that simple? We easily forget many simple things.

Instead of saying faith—one should say **faith's shade of light.** p.143,
For so it is. #257

When your whole nature, its atmosphere, has been obscured and
darkened by a life of heaping neglect and compromise—now,
where in that kind of a house could such a gay and delightful child
as Faith thrive?

The heaviest burden generous nature gave us to carry—our pride. p.145,
Only he who has been exposed to nature's generosity knows what #261
weariness is . . . But woe to him if he reaches for his liberation
through anything but this—his heaviest burden!

Engrossed. He never had the time to listen to what was said about p.147,
him. #264

Was he then in such a terrible hurry?

He sacrificed his time listening for precisely the things one cannot
grasp if in a hurry—he had no time to be in a hurry. The hustlers, oh,
they always find the time to listen for the slightest thing said of them
and to put it safely into memory—and even worse—the slightest
word they suspect is said about them.

I believe that life in the large, real life, is lived by many people—very p.151,
quietly. #275

They are not pessimists. Whoever lives his life in this vein, will not
become a pessimist. His world is too great and too deep—too quiet.

But today the world has shrunk. What makes it shrink?

"Culture." It causes eyes to dim, makes hearts numb, numb to the
grand perspective.

Rousseau was a storm warning. One day we shall have another
warning of an altogether different kind!

The end result of Schopenhauer was not pessimism but eudemon-
ism. And so it is with all the truly musical, that is, philosophical people. His pessimism was part of his system's mechanism, not the core
of his life.

Why do I "love antiquity?" Because it wakens the energies of my fin- p.152,
est needs. #278

p.155, #284 If one really desires thoughts of one's own, then one has to learn one's own brand of diligence, truly one's own; and to have no fear of being called an idler or a dreamer. Time may be money, but it is not always—life.

p.155, #285 Whoever by his nature wants (and that is to will in a great sense) least of all needs to "know what he wants." Yes, that would even be detrimental to him. He is in the same position as the artist who by no means makes it clear to his mind what is the essential secret of his strength. For he is and lives the very strength of his will.

p.156, #286 This dimness is my finest light. I know without knowing that there is my life. There everything called intention, plan, method is folly. There I am in the scheme of my nature, its method and its order. There I am soft as wax and delicate as a flower. With some luck there one day something harder than a diamond may take form in me. That would really be remarkable! All I mean is that what we call light is perhaps a strange phenomenon. "Envelop yourself in the silk of your own soul," Strindberg said toward the end of his life, when his mind was unusually clear.

p.156, #288 There exists a relationship between economy and discovery. He who has the strength to be lowly (humble) in a true sense, possesses a divining rod.

p.158, #292 Haste and fear are close neighbors, says Tacitus: slowness and hesitation are close to—firmness = *Velocitas juxta formidinem, cunctatio propior constantiae.*

p.158, #293 To prefer thought before afterthought is a most destructive diligence.

p.158, #294 How long does it take to reach that height?
If one walks slowly—four hours; if one walks fast—six.
In the most vital matters (as at the most elevated heights), this is always true. And the relation between numbers then has an even greater span!
Accidit in puncto quid non speratur in anno.[1]

[1]It happens in a moment but to hope for it takes more than a year.

With the powers of an inner sun self-effacement (*désintéresse-* ment—*Entsagung, Sich-Aufgeben*), in the great and Goethean sense— there seems to be the natural approach. This, those without sun (the people of passion), will never understand. p.166, #308

The pessimism of antiquity, as with all great pessimism, gravitates toward an inner sun.

This mystique is the mainstream never lost to Goethe. His whole richness—and the generally deplored coolness—of his external life is restrained, translucently radiant and subordinate. His fate might have been the same as a Bacon's; but his nature (inner sun) was too bright, too strong. He never had to moan, as did Bacon: "for this only I am fitted!"

Those who understand the **preparatory** importance of readiness for time are the ones who best fathom the value of time. Great bliss only needs an instant to assert itself. But the care, watchfulness, firmness, and diligence that is needed—for time to **bloom**! p.169, #314

To make an alliance with time is to ally oneself with the sun. p.169, #316

But to adopt "time is money"—indeed, then you have to turn your back on that maxim! For that is the wisdom of death and not of life.

Die Ros' ist ohn' Warum[1]: the secret of joy, power, and honor lies open (openly hidden) in those words by the great Silesian poet[2]. p.170, #318

If you harbor a spirit within you (and to admire, to love is to possess an inner animating force), it will awaken inside you that which suits the spirit. This is **learning**. p.175, #326

Genuine studying is a form of conjuration and the true fruit of having in one's soul a guest in the image of someone loved and re- vered, a guest breathing life into that inner being that can always be alive and close by him.

"Where shall I find this, how to find such a spirit?" To find is to grow morally: one never finds anything except what one is worthy of finding. Walls are covered with books; but all they secretly whisper is only this: grow!

[1]For the rose there is no "why."
[2]Angelus Silesius.

p.176, #327 You wish to be eye. But you can only see what you are; only that much, that far. You yourself are the stage and the play. *Hora vivendi: hora videndi.*[1]

p.176, #328 When eye has become lasting, when eye's decision has established itself, the ugliness of the world becomes subordinate, it loses its edge of inducement or persuasion—the edge of its slyness inherent in human wretchedness. The will of seeing transforms by its superiority, separates by covering. Eye's decision is a journey, a constantly Flowing Past. *Hora videndi* is *hora vivendi.*[2]

p.177, #330 Our relation to art (as to everything in culture's world of sublime style) brings about the same escape from the agony of civilization, the same breathing at character's higher level, conciliation, self's falling into place, as does the assuredness we feel in the greatness and solitude of untouched nature. The journey of exploration is the highest bliss, the only whole and true happiness to any being with an inherent spark of truth's life; as soon as the spirit moves, one is a Crusoe. Forest and wilderness may one day be only a tale of memory, but not even that will infringe upon the conditions of escape to nature.

p.179, #335 It is the unclearness of character—a vagueness one wishes to remain indefinite—that compels us to set our sails at strange angles. More than anything it is the courage, our "nerve" that we titillate by setting our sails cunningly. Daringly humble, humbly daring, we embark upon a dangerous course: remote—close by, far away—on a crowded route. This position is our most secure one, because it challenges our courage. Lacking an absurd position our urge would wither away, the entire scaffolding of our will would crumble. And woe to us on the day when our will for power is not—the will to effacement!

p.183, #341 The most potent energies are the gentlest; the voluntary ones *tou kairon.*[3]

Whoever wrote a book clarifying the conditions of ingenious

[1]Time to live: time to see.
[2]Time to see is time to live.
[3]the (right) moment's (energies).

energies could illustrate it with, for example, *Archimedes mousólēptos*,[1] as described by Plutarch.

I believe there is more "Jesuitism" of the finest kind in the psychology of genius than the world suspects. A character like Loyola is probably very unfamiliar, and if he is known, it is in the most unlikely quarters. Among those who knew him was Friedrich Hölderlin. But then, he also belonged to the gentle ones . . .

The true dreamers are the most realistic ones. The more hardheaded, irresistibly pragmatic—the more hidden, remote, and secret are their life's ideal, their power source of dreams, and the dream's dominion over their journey. As a result, theirs is the air of being commonplace in mysterious ways, enigmatically hardheaded; the prosaically "cynical" that is the hallmark of all forceful dreamers. They are the ones deeply submerged and engrossed in the dream. They are the ones at rest in the dream; nourished by it. The others, those who are poetically interesting, are only immersed in their own foppish fantasies. They are restless in their dreams, their souls arid and emaciated. p.186, #347

To the young the dream means very little. For they do not need their dreams. p.190, #355

My greatest days were those when my day's work was only this: to let the dream rule over me.

Voltaire—Horace. p.193, #361

The history of humanity has many bright days to hold up to the eye and human reflection, and what peculiar characteristics of such wondrous qualities there are in what a human might refer to as light and to call the bright days . . .

Once I was looking for something I could call a Menandrean world, Menandrean oases in the history of human civilization. In the life of Voltaire, in his letters at the onset of old age, I found one of the freshest, warmest of these enchantingly happy places. How drab, how dismal our most recent culture appears when compared to something of that stature—not to speak of our own Nordic culture!

[1]Seized by the Muses (spellbound).

p.195,
#364
The relation of thought-energies (interplay of inner freedom) to—not privation—but sacrifice, in the religious pureness of this concept, lies a territory where the finest attempts have been made.

Our crude worship of diligence and hard work has debased our idea of thought-energies as well as sacrifice. (Moreover, the latter concept has been practically eradicated from modern conscience.)

p.204,
#381
Submitting to physical pleasure-seeking seems to be the easiest way of yielding to hatred.

We thrive splendidly on hating one another.

There are those among us who could have been Apollos, if they had not insisted upon being Executioners at the same time. The beautiful is too delicate in nature to accept the loathsome by its side. One may hate—for the sake of love. That kind of hatred is easily recognized, even though our opportunities for observing it are limited indeed! It is recognized by the fact that it does not harm one's self.

Rivalry—The best kind is that wherein both antagonists benefit from each other, when both gain in stature. When one is wounded and falls, the other is hurt as well, even though it is not apparent.

p.206,
#384
If the serene and pure reality of a warrior nature once became clear and alive in the minds and hearts of men, wouldn't war then, what we now call war, be utterly despicable?

p.209,
#393
What is the secret of he who makes an impression?—what is his art? He can find his way to the realm of his true defenses through a rare sense that gives him strength to disregard all illusory protection.

"Is he that much richer than we are?"

"He has access to his riches!"

To accuse depletes one's strength. One cannot take advantage of one's bitterness and dangerous position, and at the same time make accusations resulting from rancor: then one lays waste to the material from which to create. This is a spellbound world! Undoing the spell is the creative task of he who possesses the word. But complaining is not the password.

The ability to endure scorn, smear, and lies with true defiance is—*eo ipso*[1]—a creative quality, leading to belief and strength—combined with the musical powers of the soul. p.214, #400

The bliss of the greatest, the Ideal, is to acquire the ability to admit one is wrong. One lives in the future, one is the future, and as such can afford to give up everything. In vain people will try to hurt you: at the moment they believe you are hit, you are not there, but far away, safe, carried in the bosom of the future. What others believe to be your dwelling and your support, totally vital to you, priceless and indispensable—the mere hint at the nonexistence of which must cause you mortal pain—you gladly threw into the sacrificial fire of your love's altar on the day when you—broken—vindicated—knelt before the Ideal. p.215, #401

There is a relationship between density, in a moral-hygienic sense, and tonality. p.216, #403
Density and solidity have their relationship to subordinacy, pressure, and utter frustration.
What is it that brings down the tone quality? It is the fact that you are not a participant in it, you are only taking part as a (profit-hungry) fake. But you are with it only in submission, under pressure and frustration: dense, whole, tone-carrying. This is the artist's "humility" with its inimitable fullness of resonance.

A strong person has an urge to admire. In that way his courage gains balance. His admiration will hardly be of the "enthusiastic" kind, but rather an appreciation wherein his soul regains its coolness, an admiration his pride longs for, by which he wants to end the feast of his day—an admiration with a cooling, subduing effect, calming like the arches of a temple. p.216, #404

Behold!—Your harsh demands upon yourself, your own true self-contempt, your rejection of and dissatisfaction with everything you had achieved: that was the solid armor that prevented the arrow p.219, #410

[1]exactly thereby.

from piercing you. In the night of your contrition there was the sunlight of secret victory, and your soul remained upright in its infamy. But now, in your frigid security—a slight gust of wind made you fall.

p.225, #422 Every situation has to be utilized. When one is spiritless—then is the spirit put to the greatest test.

p.233, #437 The most devastating of all indignation is, unfortunately, a very common one: the indignation that has secret roots in a bad conscience.

There is no doubt that this *saeva indignatio*[1] brought that terrible suffering upon Swift—no matter how resplendent its fruits. But Swift's greatness lies in having risen above this form of indignation. Therefore in his old age there is beauty after all.

p.234, #439 If you hate, it is likely that part of what you hate will stick to you. Therefore see to it that . . .

p.244, #463 A peculiar emotion that will always arise in an individual who descends into a swamp and gets stuck, is to see the accomplishment of others, and to feel as though he has been robbed.

p.261, #500 In youth it is rarely clarity that stimulates, but frequently its opposite. Could our will ever do without this stimulus? What is it that we love in clarity? Is it not its mysticism?

p.262, #501 The far-reaching, the clear and to-the-point always came from the depths of a mine. The true *hekaergos*[2] Iliadian-Apollonian was always someone with the quality of a mine—never a person of the contemporary marketplace.

Inherent in all those who had something of clarity, of coolness, of freedom to offer was the urge to flee and the sorrow of waging war. They loved power, they hated power. Out of this love, this hatred, their thirst was born: thirst for the mine and pit where the spirit could drill. This was the secret of their findings, of their divining rod.

[1]cruel indignation.
[2]far-shooting.

Ius Legendi
(The Right to Read) / 1930

Great pride yearns for suppression and humiliation. It's the Phoenix p.269 that must burn in order to live.

The duty to know who you are, fully experienced, is death to all pre- p.278 tentiousness.

There is no deeper defiance than the ability to grant that you were p.288 wrong.

    Guilt—if you place it on yourself—can give you strength and stability. If you blame someone else, it becomes not only wasted capital—it becomes the thicket, and you get stuck in its thorns.

Solid unpopularity is the only road to great influence. p.289

Selected Writings and Essays
(For the Night Falls) / 1930

p.303 What does it mean then to travel, what is it to flee?—the belief that within every misfortune hides a spice, positive to the spirit; good for perception's eye, in the long run indispensable to the will to search and discover, essential for your summer. You have made your escape; you have allowed this spice to work on you. You have fled—by staying. But the common panicky flight very often meant a harvest lost.

p.306 Silence—and good news.

I wore thin, I starved, when I got lots of news from the outside. The torrent sealed my walls to the flow of inner information, the only real source from which I could draw nourishment.

Every powerful work of the word is in a sense a first work. It took its living atmosphere from the agony and bliss of silence. But the many answers, the successes, "the honors" have often for ever deprived a writer of this atmosphere.

Bow and Lyre / 1932

Whoever shackles himself by his hankering for portliness and hun- p.15,#40 ger for power, would he have any reason to look down upon some-one who has let himself be fettered by his own vices?

That might be a good question.

What high tension of style there is in every genuine oxymoron of folk p.31,#7 tradition! The true genius of the people has always been in intimate accord with elevated style. And on translating (for example the Bi-ble!) what shrewd duplicity there is in wanting to officiously dis-solve, in an everyday manner of "style," to clarify an aphoristic high tension of the noble art with its roots in the depths of the human spirit—thus evidently attempting to approach popular under-standing!

How firm, how decidedly sure are all those everyday things of the p.89,#6 moment: conquests, practices from which see and breathe get their support. How deeply rooted: as soon as you place them firmly in focus! How close the support of closeness! How friendly the beck-oning if you heed its gesture, if you hold yourself back, if you have the courage and the will to restore your domain—*cunctando*.[1] How small, light, and inexpensive is the device needed for someone to re-gain his health, for he who loves the road deeply enough, who

[1]By deferring (Ennius about Fabius Cunctator).

loves these benevolently cunning trifles—trifles—expanding the space of will and dignity over existence, life's whole deep base of resonance.

p.150,#76 Against the impossible, the insolvable—set the impossible against—the Impossible!

Because the stature and the bearing that you grant yourself through the quest of the unattainable—that attitude is the one that protects against the most dangerous of poisonings: despair of something hopelessly beyond solution; the impossibility of your relationship to people, the impact of your life-work upon them—all hopelessly incomprehensible to them. Those who have put, as the only certainty and happiness of life, the struggle for something unattainable, have done so because they have been most ardently aware of this despair, been most profoundly burned to the bottom of their souls by something desolately insolvable, inextricable.

Traces and Signs / 1934

Light and Demands

In a profound and final analysis even the most constructive, the most p.5 positive, grows out of an anemic and wintry principle. And at the very heart of youth and soundness the word revealed itself to many: that it is always a question of possessing the talent never to be satisfied with anything but one's dissatisfaction—if at all. It is precisely such discontent that dampens the demands and makes the soul a tight vessel—in the meaning of Plato—makes it into a hermetic container that holds life within its walls: the noble confinement of summer and spirit, in healing light's safekeeping.

Eye

"The pure eye . . ." Is there no fear even in such an eye? Yes, doesn't p.6 there ultimately remain the alertness of fear—the wakefulness of *pharos*,[1] that gives light!

"The pure eye . . ." Even the brightest of the bright quivers in the reflective foil of defense's deficiencies and meanness. Even there, there is a wealth of profoundly understood and well-calculated care, as the naturally noble of a great world and a great tone seem to express themselves with the grace of indifference and freedom!

But if such calculation and cunning were the economy of our

[1]Beacon.

whole pitiful humanity's "purity . . ." would we then let go of the Ariadne-thread that shone for the eye of experience out of the half-light of so many shivering dawns!

Distance

p.15 Freedom of movement is everything. What does freedom of movement depend upon? Upon your relationship to distance.

Perhaps it is like this: the more intense your demands concerning distance, the more predestined you are for the vast movements.

I find this certain: that whoever honestly tries, honestly wants the tough, desolately barren conditions, gains access to the vast movements.

True poverty, pagan in the classical sense, mystic, evangelical, is the divining rod.

Being paralyzed

p.17 To the mind paralyzed by the darkness of night, human deficiency and ignobility may disguise themselves as the agony of bad conscience. On such occasions one has to keep the concept clear (but how difficult) that such pains should not seem alien. Their arrow had to strike at the heart, wherever you happened to be, no matter if you had been led to the most elevated position with the highest distinction in the eyes of the world; because that arrow is the thrust of your will, unquenchable. Its glowing trajectory passes through the thickest walls of man-built prestige, leveling the towers and turrets of human honors' fortress, that red hot arrow is your heart's nakedness—it is you.

But if your vulnerability should be a defenselessness without equal—by your own choice, it will be a fortress of unsurpassed strength.

p.25,#8 Fact—What is then in fact matter? Matter-of-factness? Is it not fear on one hand and love for the experience that brought Rescue on the other hand!

Is it not a fact, that these things grow so important, so ardent, so all penetrating to a person that they turn into bliss for him—and the most natural thing on earth, leaving no room in the soul for any other thought of profit than the one that is the play of life: fear—love, also called Faith.

To think ill of people is to close the road to the truth, says Sadi. But p.26,#10 has then Sadi, in all his wisdom, with all his truth, spoken less ill of people than Schopenhauer?

"Nil desperandum."[1] Character is the open door to the truth.

To grow depends upon understanding to be, to live where you are. Then all feeder streams, all sources become available to your roots. This is character. And remember he who said he had learned his wisdom from a blind man—to put his foot where it was at home. Thus you put your foot in a world.

The great hazard of life-courage!—the life-courage that is the joy of p.27,#12 reason's defensive searching power, its poetic power; the life-courage that is the Word—the word that leads and acts on humanity's journey. The great hazard of life-courage is the simple shrine of learning to be sound, to live; deeply, carefully, and with devoted comprehension. It opens the possibility to the rich and rare power of a penetrating mind's vision. Nothing is more inventive, nothing more real than true fear's lowliness.

This is demonstrated by those who have striven to enter the power of beauty, to feel and express its secret, to open avenues and byways to it for the human spirit—those who have struggled for this cause in a way accomplished by life, when driven by the hope for elimination of personal guilt and pain. This is shown by those who always remembered the great, shuddering fear and reason's deep-felt deficiency; by those who laid a foundation for the pathos of their lives and thoughts on the greatest dangers and on fleeing from them; by those who thus kept their lives and the play of their thoughts in gratitude's bright shine, chasing away all paltriness and trivia, drowning them in this warm glow. The unspeakable value of light when wordlessly understood and loved! What crushing powers this force possesses in the fight against our most treacherous enemies! Whenever has a human lived more profoundly than in the festive daylight of such convalescence?

[1] One should not despair.

p.28,#2 Where the bad conscience of a great "confessor" voluptuously combines with pretentiousness and foppery, without fail you will find an audience of upper-crust people on their knees in undisguised reverence.

It is precisely there that their craving for truth finds its full and deep satisfaction and where their passion for genuine, true sincerity has its thirst splendidly quenched . . .

p.29 This is what I would like to see in this man[1]: that there were some loci along his course where all signs distinguished him as one of those, one of great enlightenment whose lot it is to gain the right of domicile in an inviolable land. For a few moments the light of triumph touched his brow. But under the horizon dark, heavy, and evil things lie brooding, that will send a ravaging poison into his blood, make his eye stray, his step hesitant, his spirit weighted to the level of malicious enemies waiting to triumph.

Was he then so very different from the rest of us! Is he not in the midst of us now, as poisoned, as heavy, as evil and flaccid as we are! Is this where the great journey he had boasted of ended?

He did not understand (well, he understood, but not resolutely enough) that he had been tempted to relinquish his finest and most powerful gift. Now they had him where they wanted him: that is to say, on their own level.

Where should I search for him? Only there, where I know him in his greatest capacity as a writer: the blood-purifying one—only there, where I know him as direction: direction as power to give soundness.

p.30,#6 What is it inside him that hurts: that he is blamed for not having the capacities that everyone has? But adventure—deep and great adventure—has so often had a deep predestination for incapacities—misadventure.

p.33,#11 It was from his breach of faith toward himself that the passion of prosecution, wrath, and contempt took its exquisite nourishment

[1]Nietzsche.

and reached its fully grown strength. And then, while fighting the demons he himself had spawned, he was privileged to grow up to the certainty of rescue.

Why did he have to find his way to a higher form of poetry? He was looking for faith—faith and action. It is a question of belief and know-how, if he will succeed in finding an existence in the only air worth breathing: the one of believing and knowing how to believe. If not, the insanity of wrath and revenge-thoughts will devour his reason.

The prosecutor will surely be given attention. But then, it is the disposition inside us that wishes to look down, which pays attention. Education, art, strength reveal themselves in the power of understanding and that is only conceived by what is inside us craving to look up. p.35,#15

Studies—So much in this man's life seems as though it were addressed solely to myself! Contemplate the possibility that you could become a letter written for a recipient waiting somewhere in the future. p.40,#6

That joy is possible—for someone in the predicament of a human being—yes, that is a very serious matter. p.50,#18

When cheap joy pays a visit, it is great economy not to be at home, and ample reward for doing without soothing social drugs. p.50,#19

Great jesting and deep sorrow are twins, but they belong in a social world one rarely encounters.

A full day—or no day! But even the day that appears dreary may become fulfilled; dignity decides. And take heed: the day has secrets. There is territory and space in a day, in the day out there, in a day's possibility, and its traces in your mind that you haven't discovered yet, not yet interpreted. p.54,#27

Habits of living that become obstacles, and cause delay, obscuring communication between the highest degree of activity in your inner world, and your situation and actions in the outer world—these p.55,#30 habits must be abandoned. All activity in that vein is useless, no matter how clear and harmless it might appear in the light of worldly customs and their order of things—to you it will mean the highest degree of disorder. And only by separating yourself from such activity will you reach a state of peaceful communion with society.

Everything that increases the distance—thus decreasing the flexibility and the speed of your inner movements necessary to regain your integrated personality's *receptaculum*[1] where your health and defensive powers have their dwelling—you must flee. Much in the common everyday world has to be viewed in the light of this principle by a person of melancholy sensibilities, prone to irritability.

p.56,#33 Sacrificing to forgetfulness—to sacrifice with the purest blood of your will: proved to be the commandment of the day and of one's life. Because to remember faithfully, to remember with one's blood, only this will find mercy before the goddess of forgetfulness.

p.57,#34 What do we call reality, values that we live by, security?

Traces and signs of a divine life that was lost to the soul?

The lives of all seekers, lovers of reality and bliss, reach for support ultimately toward the world of these traces and signs. That is their "Rousseauism." It is the only answer they can give—ultimately—to the question: why live?

In these moments—of pureness and life—they have a light to their eyes that could be compared to the one radiating from a field in March with the sun's yellow offspring—if somebody stood up and asked: why do you bloom?

p.57,#35 What was mildness, warmth, and lee to those people? What did the choice mean to them? The choice between the mildness of benevolence, of pleasantries—and the mildness of self-restraint, alertness, and nobly vengeful sorrow. Because to avenge sorrow—one's own and others'—is a worthy deed.

p.61,#42 There is no disgrace—so singular, so individual, solely and exclusively involving you, and attached to you, that you do not share and

[1]Receptacle.

own together with everyone in the deepest sense of communion. But to this community (that is freedom) the road may be shorter and easier for you than for others, precisely by force of its solitary nature of being yours. Yes, it is from there you may rise, exactly from where it will hit you with the needle-sharp burn of singularity, at that most painfully complicated personal situation of your own and its danger point. In what you fear most lie the clearest directions for your security. Character cannot be changed; but it becomes a battlefield for powerful forces by means of vision's love, and light erupts where suffocation threatened.

Warmth . . . very good! But note that even so the road runs only and solely from your grounds, on the terms that are yours: and that all other (others') conditions are destructive to you. p.65,#49

The Greeks made all fine things into gods: even the **boundary** (*horos*).[1]

Light's **true** bactericidal action works through annihilating all that scatters and divides, all that disturbs the content of the inner life one possesses. It is the power of radiation from this **inner** sun that eradicates our enemies. It is this economy, this expansion through limitation that is the flower of light's nature. p.66,#51

Lately, more and more of Carlyle's contempt for Emerson has been publicly revealed! But did it upset the sweet twosome? No, because in Emerson Carlyle clearly saw the means of promoting his own name. And that was more important to him than any pureness of heart. Was the relationship between Strindberg and Georg Brandes any different . . . And, what indeed did Nietzsche really think about messrs Taine, Sainte-Beuve, Renan, while he so tactfully appealed to them. (One should not even speculate about what he thought of Brandes!) Yes, what an aristocrat the genius is . . . How clean the hands that preserve the fire on the altar of truth! p.70,#2

Why does man think? In order to silence the cacophony: the clamor of the will? p.74,#7

[1]Border.

Why does man think? Because thinking is a form of ownership; all else breaks on touch.

Profoundly one has to see through the emptiness of everything. But the wisest ones were those who at the same time seemed to have forgotten that they had seen through it. Where the ripest became ripe, this smile and warmth was always present.

p.74,#8 Those who came to stand for clarity in other people's minds, perhaps their secret was that (on harder, more dangerous grounds than others) they had a dual personality. And their great struggle—to the benefit and solace of others—was to be found in their constant and deeply painful choice. These people were critics, in the excruciating sense of the word. Because critique is choosing. Choice and calling; choice, cult, war.

They made "choice" a mode of life, and life their theater of operations. But the crowd, and those in power, say: "life is a battleground!" and believe they have said something important.

p.76,#5 Many a spell may be broken, many a ghost exposed if one knows how to tell them straight in the face: I have no time for you!

But it is not the question of being in such a hurry! Not to have the time for something means: to build one's living day by fulfilling it through the will to self-control!

Take one step toward—the world of "the small steps," and at once you will find yourself at the fountain of Eastern wisdom. Only in lowliness will you find no time—no time for the fear, wherein Time is wasted.

p.78,#7 But pay attention to the little things—have no fear of *akribeia*[1]—and soon you may be surprised to see that you have advanced into a larger world and that it was never any closer to you than in this rejected conscientiousness.

There is a muscle of decisive importance in your inner life that cannot be put to use and grow but through such "trifles." The roots of heroic life are not to be found up in the clouds. Do not fancy the great conquests. They are here. Here is the method of a Caesar.

[1] A sense for small things.

To place the small in a close relationship with the great: this art was the secret of people who spoke nobly and walked with dignity. That was the difference between their observance and that of the pedant. Their observance, their hygiene was—music.

Thinking of Carlyle and Emerson, of the latter's elevated and fine originality in his relationship to nature, I was sometimes struck by the fact that I could not remember having encountered any forceful streak of this kind in Carlyle. And still I felt sure that he did not lack this quality. p.83,#3

One day I read a letter written on one of his trips alone through the highlands:

> *My ride over and round Leith Hill, and through the woody solitudes—I shall never forget some glimpses there and elsewhere. Ach Gott, mein Freund! if one could speak like the Tornado, sing as the Spheres do, it were worth while breaking silence! (1840)*

There you have Carlyle's "relationship to nature!" There was no lukewarm jibberish in that relationship.

The great *sentiment d'élite*[1] which once lit in him (Nietzsche) its pure warmth: the desire to be benevolent, "the love of usefulness," the mystery of a fatherly feeling as a fulfillment of the law of beauty, unconcern about his own fate's barrenness—precisely within and through this divine Ownership (*ubi pater sum*).[2] p.87,#8

Oh, this rarity, this genuine pearl of human experience which those truly great in the realm of love and wisdom have preserved with as much care as their eye—how far he was led astray by his false grandeur of tragedy, from this feeling and the perspective of the human spirit's land which can only be attained by such feeling's mild superiority.

His life was in a way a class tragedy—the genial tragedy of class, as it often appears where you least expect it. But he possessed a strength and wisdom that are rare: to lift this tragedy, moving it up—into himself, into his innermost life; thereby making it truly representative— p.88,#9

[1]Feeling of superiority.
[2]Where I am the father.

thereby winning part ownership in it—*ius legendi*[1]—there, where the ideal of humanity is being decided. The advantage of suspicion lies for him in its burning inducement of the connection to Apollo-Hygieia, illuminated by one of the warmest, most secretive spirits of exploration. This physical, moral disposition—his evil and his good one—constituted his whole possibility to become eye, eye's deep struggle and desire. It was what placed him beyond, and where he had to find his salvation. This was his character and how well he recognized it. How well he deciphered its most concealed wording and its most secretive understatements, found everywhere in the history of the human heart where someone who was branded stamped his insignia!

p.89,#10 It is the great instinct of poetry and art that comes to light in Nietzsche when all his search converges, secretly—adventurously in the hope for the perfect climate. That is the great artistic quietism (*Lauterkeit*)[2] which was the Germanic principle of soundness in his nature—that quietism that in this game of instinct and calculation, in his later days attempts to assert itself, to govern and lead.

p.89,#11 He created his philosophy out of the conditions for his physical clarity.

His whole philosophy could carry the heading: My Climate.

Eventually, a future climate of humanity shone before his eye, but then he seems to have lost the measure applicable to the conditions of the present. His health (illusory) confused the vision. As long as he was on his way to his climate, his recovery, his eye had sureness. In reality he could only live as a convalescent. Maybe Epicurus was more like him than anyone else in this respect. But the distinctiveness of this feature is far from unusual in the characters of the philosophers of antiquity!

Eros—Virtus

p.90,#1 *Hybris*[3] and Eros belong together. Both blossom in the most fruitful and fecund unison from the effemination, shrinkage of the intellec-

[1]The right to read.
[2]Purity.
[3]Overconfidence.

tual urge for purity. Plato rejects the common Eros, even the artistically "inspiring," and the only one he recognizes is in effect the one (believe it if you have the strength) who extinguishes the other. Yes, Plato is truly refreshing when you consider the whole mess of the sentimental modern techno-psychological Eros which is now so nobly, pitiably practised on the enigmas of the ingenious spiritual life . . .

Life, worth, human dignity were never more at stake than in the characters who at the core of their Eros experience departed from time, environment, and general sanctions. Therefore you sometimes find the most intense, the rarest, the strongest ambitions and the greatest vulnerability in these personalities. In the ingeniously religious ones, this grows to something else that appears to be (and perhaps also is) the opposite—because with them it is a must: in order to save the personality from disintegration. p.93,#4

Nothing is more real, nothing more impossible than the thought. p.97,#5
    On one condition the impossible becomes reality: that you are capable of placing yourself in a living relationship to it.

To wake by secret conjuring, to evoke by the casting of spells—that is to idealize (reality awakening, reality arousing—"reality's rendering"). p.97,#6

The noble world of the common people that Almquist[1] wanted to illuminate, disclose, and establish against the world of so-called culture . . . would have been his salvation, if he had really possessed the self-mastery to humble his life. This noble element was present in every great poet—and its incompatibility with the "bourgeois culture," with the distortion of civilization—became the tragedy of their characters. I do not see it any differently in Almquist—than in Burns. What stroke of luck a character like Thoma[2] represents with his certain and clear politics! So much of such fortunate vision has been implied in Almquist's character—it secretly whispers in "the Painter" with so much foreshadowing anxiety! p.98,#8

[1] 19th century Swedish author.
[2] German painter (1839–1924).

The Second Light / 1935

p.18,#30 What then may a human being finally have to say about himself?
I was man—child and fool—as any human being.

Under certain conditions, you even have to accept, yes, enter into alliance with your moments of darkness, your follies. How else would you be able to absorb what you call—your wisdom?

p.22,#39 A critic—if he does not belong to the backwater school—has to know more than others about the prerequisites of humankind, about its growth and health and the economy of these conditions. He must possess strength and energy of experience in order to clearly define such conditions: a pure definition of the atmospheric prerequisites of the human species. He has to be one person, of one spirit—of *one* music and criticism. Then he may become the one who solves, reveals, and liberates.

This great vision could give inner glow and inner plan to a pragmatic search within the coexisting past, sacredly alive—

mál ok manvit
ok laeknishendr. —[1]

But this forest is no woods of past years and data, psychopathic "facts" and literary psychology and anecdotal gossip. Therefore it was rarely entered.

[1]Eloquence and good sense and healing hands (from the Edda).

Our right to the value of our life—to become a source of warmth, a p.29,#57
power of reality, a discovery of value for others—depends upon
quiet, gray, and simple things; stronger, more precious than anything "tragic."

He who has placed himself in true relation to his adequacies does not p.49,#13
need to enter into any relationship with his inadequacies.

To be properly engaged in what befalls you would result in a lack of
time to engage in what does not befall you. And this is exactly the
true adequacy.

The main thing is not—that is the strange situation of man—that a p.61,#42
wound heals: but that it is kept clean! An open wound is something that happens constantly.

What is content? That light is shining. p.95,#36
And the condition for this—namely that the air is clear—that is
what we call form.

Where you confide in form, you will meet no danger. If you confide deeply—deeply enough.

A poet is someone belonging to the primitive class of people, or he is p.95,#37
no poet. A poet is given to passion's character, that is, spirit's character: in the extreme line of probability.

The joy of the poet lies in his sense of reality, in his passion for reality.

A poet is either someone who unveils, or he is the opposite: someone p.96,#41
busy patching up his veil.

Honor is to feel like future. He who "relishes honor," gorges himself p.110,#77
precisely on the muck of today. Honor is always a futurity: and as
such it can never be the object of enjoyment. And—there is a profound sentence—only rarely proven: to die for one's honor.

In the sting of beauty—and its proper pain—yes, there much can be p.151,
decided. In the sting of beauty—your feeling is straightforward and #168
simple, you see fully and without fear, that it is right to say that

wrath, anger's envy, and all that may be called a "sick eye" is outside "the chorus of the divine." Yes, in the sting of beauty—and its proper pain—that is where you light the torch, where the men of the great procession have always lit their torches, by the statue of Eros.

p.177, #231 "The loneliness of those who give." No and yes! To give is really—an art: an art that does away with all simple loneliness. Only by virtue of getting everything for free can you become someone who gives. Only someone who receives can give.

p.177, #232 "The loneliness of those who give." That is surely the proper sentence . . .

But still, he was so far from the self-evidence of this wisdom and thus its healthy character, he was not magnanimously and freely youthful enough for this wisdom; no, he was too harsh, too untried, too youthful for this wisdom.

p.178, #233 Nietzsche did not give himself enough time to digest his food, in other words—to experience. Thus his many Tartufferies, his intentional and unintentional treacheries, his unfaithful surrender to the enemy of what had been most sacredly entrusted to him. He began with the noble Titans, those of the bow and lyre, the Titanic forces of the Muses—and wound up with the apprentices.

Nietzsche did not allow himself time for experience. In other words: he was not what he so proudly believed himself to be—a psychologist. The very fact that he brags about being one gives him away . . .

p.179, #236 The true giver is lonely as a child: childishly lonely—together with light.

p.183, #244 It was the Titan in its purity that he wanted to reenact. "Restore in man—peace, greatness, simplicity." But a poverty of heart never satisfied, never soothed and appeased, constantly threw him into the arms of avarice. And his greediness made him abuse the music of his nature—his nature's asclepiadical music. He began with noble Titans—and what a hint of fate it is that finally, the names that follow him are those of Strindberg and Brandes.

All I have seen—in history and culture—has made me doubt that a great man, not even what we call a man of great spirit, can ever be something beautiful. p.185, #250

No, a little human being, the child, is the most beautiful creature one may see in this world. And, then, perhaps someone who resembles a child.

Firmness and journey: whereby dream and knowledge (life effort) join hands—thought takes advice and nourishment from dream, to direct oneself in such a way. p.208, #301

So many good words I have heard in dreams that I later only had to write down. I am as certain about the experience of this road of knowledge as any Pythagorean, and I believe that human existence under such a controlling element might some day arrive at a more solid life doctrine than through all rules of reason.

"The eye of the master makes the horse fat," but many were taught a harsher lesson . . . that only the firmly watching eye has the capacity to make a tiger listless; that in the absence of this eye he will secretly fill himself with might; and when we return from our forgetfulness, our distraction and "inhalation," he throws himself upon us and maims us beyond any defense. p.209, #302

The wisdom of the aging has one, only one remedy: converging vision. p.213, #310

For anyone with a conscience ill at ease, all that his eye catches—a bird, a dog, a tree—lies in the stinging sign and memory of good conscience's light. Often I have wondered whether the power to perceive the beauty of the world was secretly related to a sick conscience. The closer I came to the enigma of beauty, the closer was the enigma of guilt. p.224, #334

What lacks *ēthos*—is thrown off balance—is unerringly characterized by this: that something beautiful that was captured, seen, and remembered, causes pain. There are infinite degrees of this pain. Perhaps it is never fully gone.

ēthos—kairon:[1] my concern with fundament and light.

[1]Evenness of mind—constructive moments.

p.228, #342 The purest and most profound human beings have lived, thought, dreamed: the mystique of faith—and the breach of faith.

And thus they have dreamed up—man.

Because *stirb und werde* (die and become) in all its heroism is still nothing but the sworn sign of the best and finest aspect of human longing—estrangement's call of faith out of the abyss.

p.231,#1 In regard to physical pain, as well as to the onrush and storm of thought, there is one way and relationship (method) to combat them by not offering resistance. The love of the awareness of a protective haven at the core of every human soul, which throughout life has sacrificed to hope, is eventually the only possession that lasts. And no greater sentence than this has been uttered in this world: "*That ye resist not evil*" (Matt. 5:39). This is a flower whose brilliance reaches the heavens and whose light tears apart the gates of hell.

My whole composition—for life's work and the day: my right to make sacrifice to hope: to serve and stand fast in order to be able to make sacrifice to hope.

p.231,#2 Experience is limitless, that is—limitless as Faithfulness.

Experience is rare, rare as Faithfulness. Experience's greatest adventure will eventually be to find the part of one's conscience, where the hunger for true relation contains the certainty of truth and its security, eliminating every thought of a possible distortion.

Therefore: make hunger the subject of your studies.

p.242,#28 Mercilessly clear information about the road traveled, about humankind with its disgrace and shame startle the eye of the aging. But age also has a kind of mild, soft distinction to distract the altogether too harsh light, to shed over the sharp furrows, the creases of the spirit, the cheap and coarse ones—distinctions of a nobler class.

Elpidi / 1939

Whoever inherited plenty may blame luck—unless his nature has p.5,#1 much of that which compels strong personalities to prove their right to inherit.

To master a subject, a task; to achieve the power of vision to create p.5,#3 and mold: only by force of—the will to pay which constitutes your life-style's *enkráteia*[1] and border sentinel, perceived in the context of life by purest experience. It is in the willingness to pay that a person finds his worthwhile pieces of information that exclusively transform into blood and lasting power. And in this experience lies the *punctum saliens*[2] for all life-style of substance.

Only he who owns can give things name. The task of the poet, in a p.7,#7 sublime sense, may be cloaked in the mystique of naming things: the lusterless congruity—the Olympian lowliness, its concord of to know and to be.

A voluptuously peaceful and quarrelsome—succulently placid and p.9,#11 gossipy
       suave mari magno[3]. . . !
how often is this—and nothing else—the whole purpose of our so-

---

[1] Self-control.
[2] The crucial point.
[3] It is gratifying to watch the open sea (and the winds stirring the surface, to watch from the shore somebody else's great toil) (Lucretius).

called historical experience! The glee of tradition, talebearing glee: "humanism!"

Even Dante was a learned man! But for sure—between him and his "teacher" (Brunetto) lies a tempest—a storm of purity, a fury of sorrow, a misology—to the liking of Plato.

p.13,#17 The Swedish word for the character of a Coriolanus is: *ovidlådenhet* (*unattachment*).

The Latin version—in crystalline manliness: *solutus omni foenore*.[1] But an unattachment without brittleness is something beyond the human.

p.13,#18 Behind Shakespeare's *Coriolanus* there is perhaps the wonder and silence of an awesome critique: a silence of the same kind that once made Plato halt as though before something enigmatic, something "adventurous," as he calls it, before the question: whether, within virtue itself, contrast and antagonism reveal themselves: the silence of a culture concept that in spite of all seeks support and foundation in the great vision and experience—the one that rises above all "tragic" cheapness—that the straighter the attitude, the more flexible the person.

p.15,#23 Aporia[2] and adventure! Where this ends remains but the common muck—and asphyxiation.

There are those who fled and suffocated—by believing that they succeeded! Stimulus of spirit: keeping it holy (without all "prompting!")—that is the perfection of the art of living.

Aporia and adventure: Whatever to the world, in your case stood out as ignominious and ill-fated—in times of darkness—could be the foundation for the great possibility of the approach: of becoming pure, sharp, clear. And the more you will feel in your nature its representative power, right and validity of human history, the more fruitful you will find your reconciliation in the joy of clarity—overcoming—by means of this background.

To have things brought to a climax—even self-rejection—perhaps therein lies redemption.

[1] Free from all usury (Horace).
[2] Predicament.

Animi concordia[1]—where you have the principal pattern "in poten- p.16,#24
tia" even in failure—you have not, "in factu," failed! Yes, such reality may be a feast for the will—while frequently, in success there is
torment: pressure, skinlessness.

Someone who in his character has a compelling incentive to make p.17,#26
poverty—in all its significance—down to the clearest foundation!—
his subject of study, his research and his plan, and perhaps then even
in the hopes of bringing his life and his journey in par with the light
radiated by this research—he has an adventure to live for as great as
that of any hero.

The great mistake: to consider poverty, lackluster, lowliness as a
purely religious and mystical concern! The deeply pragmatic, worldly side of poverty's flexible and bright euphoria: the point is to bring
precisely its entire depth of significance into the spirit.

The profit urge: wholly and fully to make the subject of boldest expectation—altruism!—the unselfishness that has conceived its goal,
its determination through the experience that a person is really only
growing according to the measure of adroitness and nonconcern in
the attitude toward the world and gain he is capable of mustering in
his life: egotism of the thought and the joy of thought.

But no tarnishing, no disgrace can backfire more readily than taking p.18,#27
credit for a merit.

"Wie kann es mir gleichgültig sein" (How can I be unconcerned)—
exclaims Hamann—*"dass man an der Celebrität meiner Eitelkeit arbei-
tet, wenn ich selbst dem Gefühl der Vernichtuhg unterliege"* (that the focus of attention is the celebration of my vanity, when I myself am
subjected to the feeling of annihilation)—If he only had had that
strength! (If he in spirit and truth had possessed the power of this
devastation, of this annihilation.) Then he would also have possessed all that he was capable of owning, that which was purest and
strongest: because the power of this destruction is a force. It was the
agony of asphyxiation due to the lack of this power that now tor-
mented him.

This has been secretly whispered everywhere! —The noblest atmosphere was created out of the most ardent thirst; the upholding of

[1]Concord of the soul.

this condition gave relief to the thirst! —From each attempt to slake, solace this thirst, exclusive of these conditions for creation, anxiety is born as well as exclusion from the flow of nourishment of the noblest breathing organ. How clearly and openly this has revealed itself! Probably no less in the case of a Nietzsche than in a Hamann? —"Can you now see to it that my seclusion, my poverty is restored!" It was this motion, this artifice of child and spirit—child and giant—that he could no longer perform. Then the fire consumed him.

p.21,#31 Make a man hanker—make him take the credit for his merit, his "honor"—and soon he is devoid of strength, excluded, a nonperson! The relationship with reality has been dislodged. As a result the entire human function is disturbed.

It is our instinctive awareness of this that manifests itself in us as a secret malice (and consolation!) when we see a person being honored.

It is in the clarity of this function that the surprisingly open and simple conceptions of antiquity's power has its foundation, and not least its great and real evaluation of—the concept of honor.

p.22,#32 *Elpidi*[1]—No other reward, no other prize for victory than Hope. —As soon as one can position oneself to live—one stands before a light of beginning, before a *theion pragma*[2] of exploration's spirit, knowledge, direction.

—"For those who are capable of this, the world is good."

p.27,#40 *"Ti scongiuro, Nolano, per il divino tuo genio, che ti difende et in cui ti fidi, che vogli guardarti di vili, ignobili, barbare et indegne conversazioni; a fin che non contraggi per sorte tal rabbia e tanta ritrosia, che . . ."*[3]

On a golden tablet—on the golden tablet of conscience these words by Giordano Bruno (from "Cena delle Ceneri") should speak to every heart that has felt the peril of wrath. A Tegnér would have been spared many "tiger hunts" if he had been able to carry through such a plan!

[1] To hope. ("Sacrifice foremost to hope." Theognis)
[2] Divine deed.
[3] "I beseech you, as a townsman of Nola, by your divine genius, who defends you and in whom you confide, that you beware of base, crude and barbaric conversations; not to have fate bestow upon you such ire and dour obstinacy, that . . ."

Oh yes, whoever can carry out this scheme and solve this great question of relations (question of sustenance and correlation!)—even if he should lose out on every spectacular "result"—he still would have gained life!

The weaker, the more irresolute your attitude toward spirit and its demands, the more you condemn, lament, accuse. In the most intense fields of energy, on the road of pure war, you have no other adversary—no one else to judge but yourself. In the high tension fields of energy you always pass judgment from such pride of joy's lowliness, always—from below.   p.28,#44

Where it was possible to establish insight and confidence in that relationship; there in the sensitivity to feel pain, the lowliness, the lee of the wind have been allowed to form; where the warmth and magic of lackluster have been given their possibility: there the most healing of all human radiation—and a gratefulness to fate would be gained, endowing the strength to carry one's conditions. In all real action lies the power of reflex action. In action—retroaction. Only in victory will you learn what art of arms you practised! Whoever has become a significant factor to others, shall feel significance grow: truth—and love of fate.

Eris and *āskēsis*.[1] He who keeps his wound clean also makes envy clean!   p.32,#50

Taste makes a good and secure bridge from one human to another: between loneliness and loneliness. Taste is a continuous feast of friendship.   p.56,#41

Mnemosyne[2]: Faithfulness to the first lights, to the early stage of a perception.   p.91,#17
   The noblest kind of alertness will prove to be the one, which in the final analysis has not concentrated on capturing time, but rather—the timely earliness.

In taste there is one development, one evolution: Newness. Precisely for that reason it has nothing to do with news.   p.96,#30

[1]Contest and observance.
[2]Greek mythology: the goddess of memory, mother of the nine muses.

All radicals—from Plato to Comte—have agreed that news ruins taste.

Precisely because newness, perceived in the sanctity of passion—newness of life—is their most precious treasure.

p.97,#32 Life's strength is not to be found in any violent outburst; its uniqueness and novelty lies embedded in a fresh, coarse evenness.

In the eye unsmudged by all results: there youth is proving itself, there it is sustained.

Basically it is our greed that forces us to err against the great time relationship, the love relationship: Time.

To learn to die for Time—is to live: to be a true unfashionable.

What lasts and lives is—with all its firm outline: the eternal feminine—the flower-softness.

p.98,#34 Allusion may be a withered intellect's last artifice and aid. Allusion may be a torch— and tall as art.

p.98,#35 *Acroamen paucis!*[1]

A "broad audience" is an abomination. It has never existed, cannot be.

p.98,#36 The most absurd of all challenges—but the one for ever sure of victory: a radicalism in taste.

p.98,#37 One cannot live for anything but war, *hoc est*[2]—taste:

and there is no other honor to strive for than that of being declared someone redundant, where nothing is more redundant than—*to dikaion tēs Mousēs.*[3]

p.98,#38 *Macte nova virtute, puer*[4] (Virgil) —But these good wishes are in reality the absolute ones! Only he who stands at the Beginning—*nova luce*[5]—is to be felicitated.

p.99,#2 The best movement: the one that grows out of an urge for density—in the relationship to yourself and your day—which in turn by its

[1]Delight for the ears of a few.
[2]That is.
[3]The bliss of the Muses.
[4]Hail to thee, my boy, for your new (young) virtue (Virgil).
[5]In the new light.

own force gives birth to freedom of movement—while the mobility
you get for free, very often cuts down the need for density, and thus
becomes useless.

The day itself—the best poem! But it has to be dense. Dense—like
any good poem.

All poetic activity emanates from the urge for density: thus rein- p.100,#3
forcement, protection—growth of skin and from the experience that
what endangers life also constitutes its essence—that you outwit the
danger by remaining in it, taking a stand: that you duplicate the
danger, waste the possibilities of finding firm ground, protection and
reinforcement by taking the opposite course, the course of diversion.

To live poetically is to densify life.

At a certain point, the experience becomes most outstanding, when p.100,#4
ways and means and substance flow from each other, move within
one another. Nothing but your conscience-relationship to what you
have experienced as density, as imperviousness, creates protective
skin. A man of experience always professes—and has to confide
in—the *l'art pour l'art* principle.

Where experience becomes tentacles groping for assurance—
where this truth and method consolidates itself and becomes stability: there lies a person's real growth, expansion, and self-command.

Form: our deepest instinct of protection. It is a question of form p.101,#5
without support—whether that will open up for you, that will
envelope you which is the protective power of form.

"Di bene fecerunt, inopis me quodque psilli finxerunt animi, raro et per- p.102,#7
pauca loquentis." (Hor. *Serm.*–I.4)[1]
The profession and art of the sayers—insofar as passion is involved,
namely the art of those who did not seize the pen unless their aim
were a life expression of the fullest pregnancy—must by all necessity
lead to a search for the laws of human economy. Their acquisition of
character (the art of channeling life) is the process of the fruit ripening, growing transparent from self-knowing: self research beyond

[1]"The gods did well who made me poor and insignificant at heart, rarely speaking and
in few words" (Horace. *Serm.*–I.4).

the conditions of limit and distance necessary for liberation of the most blissful energies. They are all *perpauca loquentes*[1]: lapidaric—and expansive.

The great voyages of exploration have been undertaken *in nuce* (at the core)—"In a nut-shell"—says Shakespeare-Hamlet. And the true, joyous light of an *aphorismēnon*—is also exactly what the word says: the one of separateness.

If, of all literary forms, the aphorism is the one most profoundly limited, this would also indicate that—in order to have any meaning—it is also the most profoundly limiting form and as such precisely—unlimited.

p.103,#8   The smallest sum of pure desire—is better than any gross amount of a mixture! That is Plato's sentence in *Philebos*—and it is the cardinal maxim for productive economy and life consistency. Because he who adapts his existence to the sum of such things will soon learn that his other, everyday, and common ways must become a bridge between them. And that is how all true fullness of life is created. Anything else is illusion of relationship—plans, but never plan. Because plan is not, as in the eye of the crowd, the cult of strength and power. It goes deeper: it is the cult of life's fullness.

p.103,#9   There exists no other *deinótēs*[2] than the straight line. The diligence of antiquity is the desire to condense. Intensity, swiftness, brevity. *Linea brevissima.*[3]

p.105,#13   Politics, under the eye of Minerva—of the Eumenides![4] The more passionately (the more dangerously) you experience the distortion of humankind, the more passionately you have to direct your hope toward the field and sanctuary where, by the highest degree of willingness, in companionship and under the eyes of Minerva—and the Eumenides—you possess knowledge.

The *ananke*[5] of art: the mystical point—for illumination and

[1]Speaking in few words.
[2]Striking force.
[3]The shortest line.
[4]The Furies (Greek mythology).
[5]Necessity.

guard—where freedom and compulsion to prove oneself become one.

It is on freedom all art leans; it is freedom all art teaches.

To be wise enough, tranquil enough, noble enough to give priority to joy . . .

But this is play!

It is not only play, it is grace. And grace is only achieved by—legitimacy.

The more clearly exacting, the more unpopular the artistic aim—the more important the demand for clarity! p.108,#17

It is the passion for explicitness and clarity that predestines the work of an artist to unpopularity. Basically only clarity is truly and implacably unpopular.

Real subtlety has no other warmth, no other "constructiveness" than openness and evenness. If you want to work and be—you cannot chase after swaggering pomp. Even hard teeth are not strong enough for the solid truth.

Nothing is more personal, more original, closer to one's self, than clarity. It is easy to keep track of the exceptions! But only the most exceptional are well-versed in what is generally valid, open, and clear.

The trait of ancient Norse poetry in a Whitman—from his innermost p.123,#2 experience, a self-determined, cynically[1] simple *sub divo*[2] revealed itself through the intimately proven practice of the grand ancient spirit: a trait of the ancient Norse bard such as it documented itself in his poetic work, his striving for a pragmatically illiterate, pure rendering of life and form—that is valuable in Whitman.

Whitman foresaw a new classicism. He was a nuisance to the learned. And a liberator—for the innocents.

The truly good expression is not only, as Lichtenberg says, tanta- p.130,#1 mount to good thought—it is a dire necessity that sooner or later will make its forceful entrance. And nobody has a surer road than he who has his pathos of thought tied to a great love of language—the language's own fullness of promise and power of conquest.

[1]In the original Greek sense (Kynikos).
[2]Under open sky.

p.131,#3 You will have no part of language's treasure of truth unless you deliver yourself to the reality of your inner experience. The source was always found in this simple, naked expression of productive, basic, relationship characteristic of the ancients—a relation of simplicity to the word, hunger and thirst to express: be beneficially plain-spoken. Poetry and mysticism are true defenders of the language, its noble life.

p.131,#4 In the world of language sources of power often exist where the scientifically trained mind least of all suspects them. And anyone who uses the language to trace and close in on life's relationship to reality in spirit and thought—*pharmaca phobou*[1]—drinks the heart blood of language.

In antiquity such instinct of language was the origin of the greatest poetic art. Still, during the Middle Ages generous and sensitive popular tradition granted Virgil this character and rank.

p.141,#11 That "time is money"—that outcry of morons—requires an inner translation. It is Time, in the context of density, of rhythm, of the ability to sustain and receive, which is "money" and—more than that— also heals. It is this omnipresent power of wholeness, that we so easily let pass us by.

p.179,#31 In younger years, when I noticed how great characters such as Darwin and Schopenhauer doubted the possibilities of human dignity, I was indignant.

But everything human is fragmented. Not even Plato himself was always dressed for the music he spoke of.

The hero—no matter his eminence, and no matter our paltriness, still needs our indulgence.

p.199,#21 The secret of all art is to lead us into the borderland of the human and the divine. Whoever can remain an inhabitant there—make use of the border—can become a channel of communication, a donor.

[1]Medicine against terror.

Concordia Animi / 1942

All self-experience lacks glossiness. Only what you pilfer glitters— _{p.7,#1} stings your eyes. The open words are never the "new," the conspicuous ones. They remain in the lustreless low-key of eternal archaism. There is a silence around all simple inexhaustible things. To make this silence felt, heard, is art, wisdom.

Everything mortal expresses defenselessness. It is just as clearly in- _{p.59,#92} scribed above the head of a young bird as above the skull of a human petrified by evil and stupidity. But it requires great spiritual strength to see the likeness and the correlation in it. And it is not always the one who sees that has his day.

Can I determine what I want to recall to mind: revive my property _{p.74,#11} and right to it? Is it not so that I must concentrate my life on the highest level of recognition, because I have experienced in the mirror-depth of conscience, that all teachings and advice useful to me have to be physically self-evident, physically recognizable: as though by my whole being—recalled?

Imagination is the power to discover—by force of being rooted. _{p.111,#13} Imagination, as revered by the crowd: ingenuity—by force of being rootless.

p.164,
#168
"The tongue of the just is as choice silver."[1]

The fact that truth obeys the laws of the muses: there Greek thought was on the heels of something tremendous.

p.195,
#228
In the human mode of expression (what might be called world literature) there exists a secret Middle Kingdom, which only the very few have had an eye and an ear sensitive enough to recognize—the true sanctuary of the literary art, beyond any confessions and policies. Every pure expression, every autómaton,[2] *integrum*, springs from recognition; is in the highest and warmest sense: criticism.

[1](The Book of Proverbs 10:20.)
[2]Spontaneous; something happening naturally, as when wild flowers grow.

Atticism—Humanism / 1943

A sense of experience suffocated in sarcasm—by pampering of will, p.7,#6
by the ruminating of wishfulness . . . what else constitutes the history of most "gifted" people! How little room in a human life for that
sacredly inopportune, that great rarity: joy!

A pathology never disproven—always favored by youth: that the en- p.7,#7
viable in spirit is what is sound! The more impossible a situation, the
richer in—possibilities.

"Wisdom with a heritage" . . . Where is the salt that preserves? To p.7,#8
feel the necessity of defense. The religiosity itself is but an awareness
of, an exposure of—profound joy. The right exposure is the protective salt. The right salt is the surest heritage.

The best polemics: to speak up and dare, and still, within, chal- p.8,#10
lenging—oneself.
    "*Indignatio facit versus*"[1] . . . But the strongest poetry that exists is
the one of the eye. Many a lover of what is direct and pure, many a
good person contemptuous of all that is cheaply tepid and stifling,
still eventually lets himself be pampered by—his wrath!

The world of wrath is the world of the common. Those who thank p.8,#11
you there are the ones fundamentally without strength: the com-

[1]Indignation makes verses (Juvenal).

mon ones. But those who deeply and honestly suffer in the world of wrath—they are the strong ones; and they are refreshed by an entirely different word! Their judgment grows, their taste lasts.

p.9,#12 Where do you encounter the cleanest weapons?

They belong to those who had to muster the most profound cunning—to wrench the weapons out of their own hands.

p.10,#18 The probable fundamental taste.

—Only in the incomparable is there a muscle that grasps—and a conquest for freedom. A virus always sticks to taste. Where the test is—there is also certainty: unwavering taste!

It is the connective agents that are to be considered the foremost ones. He who has the clearest concept here, has an Archimedean point and—home. But connective agents can only be produced from something that burns, something bitter. And there should be the howling of storm around a home! Roof over the head and quiet you have only in accepting something inextinguishably, inexhaustibly—caustic.

A great love of vision cannot exist nor last other than under conditions of an extraordinary connective element. It is essential here not to become confused by any (genial or half-genial) sophistry. What is enviable always lies beyond the heart's counterfeiting.

Expanse of wings: *res angusta!*[1] Only in the incomparable will there be a muscle that grasps, *deinótēs*[2]—cloudlessness. Without the stigma of something exceptional—there will never be a *hors concours,*[3] never a home of one's own! I believe that those without a homeland have been the ones who had the best ear for the music, for the taste that creates home for a human being.

p.17,#28 There seems to be a discontentment with oneself, in the absence of which, literally and spiritually, one cannot digest one's food. Perhaps this condition is the basis for all living sense of culture, all finest taste.

[1]Res angusta (domi) = Narrow circumstances (at home).
[2]Striking force.
[3]Out of the competition.

The friendship with oneself—the cardinal condition for human happiness—seems to be dependent upon a certain talent—never to be satisfied with oneself.

Yes, with cynical frankness a straightforward poet, Ewald von Kleist   p.21,#38
(Frederick the Great's general), dared to utter these words:

> *Ein wahrer Mensch muss fern von*
> *Menschen sein.*[1]

And not only Schopenhauer—but even the "humane" Schiller have praised him for those words! It would be hard to find such courageous poets (not to speak of generals)—in our time of busybody socializing.

Are there any worse thieves than the big hug—the popular confi-   p.21,#40
dence . . . "be on a good footing with people!"

Social intercourse without a refined rivalry will hardly do, will not   p.22,#41
go far. But what is rivalry but—seclusion! These paradoxes can be traced wherever art has grown. Much depends upon the wise insight into the importance of outer paradigms to which one in the final analysis is not yet subservient.

Even with the good-humored, "those pure at heart," it is sometimes   p.22,#42
easy to note that the natural and courageous joy in knowing that you have the educated unity of the whole mass against you, has given the urge for condensation and density the sting and virus of—malice, not reprehensible from a human standpoint!

How will you prepare yourself for flight if not by a no to everything   p.23,#44
that is "stone inside your wing!" The ascetics are right: the things worthy of experiencing in this world depend upon that "no" (the "no" of the question of contour—of expansion) that rids the wing of its stone. There is nothing more worthy of experience than freedom. It is not possible to endure the revelation of human servility's repulsiveness except by the wing of flight (*penna fugiente*): in one's power of vision and search.

[1] A true human being must be at a distance from people.

p.24,#46 Who is freer from all worries of relationships than he who must make art into life, life into art—where will one find a more splendid necessity than this: to prove oneself only in the thought of art!

p.25,#48 The human being: a border phenomenon? Its ultimate bliss, its ideal seems to be nothing but this: to be—anxious in a joyous way.

p.26,#52 **The free hands!** Whoever is forgotten has something great to gain—time. Even where fame has become an incitement to "utilize time," it has nearly always become a loss of time, a theft of time, a fatal nature. If something belongs to the world of Muses, wholly and irrevocably—it is the pure concept of time. An uncompromising idea of time (the noble concept of time) can never be kept alive accompanied by everyday occurrences.

p.27,#53 **The celebrated penitent** is an apparition of ridicule to gods and men—something devastatingly bitter to himself. It should be the privilege of only the more recent culture circus to let such a misfit appear.

p.28,#56 No doubt there is a force that creates warmth of the greatest value to personal joy, as well as a productive measure of proliferation in a purposeful direction toward a small group of people with experience of taste and culture; people sharp-sighted and devout, at the same time deeply disappointed and profoundly hopeful—consciously neglecting every thought of making an impression as far as the world marketing of culture throughout the cacophony of the day is concerned. In order to build and maintain such a living atmosphere of thought and art (dietetics, regimen), one should search for a way to study there vividly and with the glow of exploration the force of search, the rare fate of exceptional men, the tragic and exclusive eras of refinement on the stage of the thought and the heart—**the life philology.**

p.30,#58 Nothing as honest, nothing as matter-of-fact—as the fleeing! There is no other fellowship than the one based upon purest solitude. What else comes to light in art, taste, style! What is the force that creates ideals other than the need for a land set apart and untrodden, an *au de là?*[1] And precisely thus it has meaning, purpose, and usefulness. Even the "civic" world needs this salt. Many a sly fox of togetherness carries a burning envy. He knows well enough on whose side youth stands—"Beauty young and free"—that is exclusively the forum (scarce and rare) where honor and future are decided!

To Marcus Aurelius, as to the Indians, the perfect course of action be- p.31,#61 comes complete self-effacement. Only to those who look at the exterior, those without a center, there is "privation." *Ne te quaesiveris extra.*[2] Much in Marcus Aurelius really belongs in the same world of knowledge as the *Bhagavad Gita*. It is strange how this perspective is both open and—closed. But the Indians have been "lacking a skin" much more than the Greeks—and Greek Romans!

It is certainly not the people of coexistence's joy nor the ones of sti- p.32,#63 fling cordiality who have been the source of the most ardent spirit and—alliances! No, those of an entirely different stock: those who have been most ardently burnt in what has been called spiritual friendship, by the gust of wind from a—never here! Burnt by the longing for a haven and communion, whose maxim is an eternal: carry on! How the spirit in such clarity of vision is capable of empathy and insight into the minds of those constantly torn by social dependence and illusions!

It is by the ability to ask questions one defends oneself. When that p.33,#64 power (and the one of suspicion) has dried up—you stand without a weapon.

There probably always have existed people able to admit to themselves that with their enemies they have basically felt comfortable, but with those in harmony of recognition—fundamentally never. Does not the privacy of the strong ones demand lack of understanding? Is it not rather like the ceiling of clouds that prevents the warmth to escape from the earth? Is there any coldness superseding the one created by the illusion of communion!

[1]A beyond.
[2]Do not venture outside (of yourself).

p.36,#69 To reach the best motifs: precisely by the force of—what stings the most! It is then that the art of "titillation" counts. Plato surely knew . . . And because he knew this better than all poets, it follows that this great, fastidious man—shunned poetry.

p.37,#71 **The great thought of fleeing**—there exists something rushed through by wind—the wind of spirit—where every wish is despised. On the level of Plato, in the direction of radical taste, lie wonderful distances, untrodden paths and retreats . . . new land—only divined by the few!

May forests and wilderness die . . . flatness take over everything! Whoever was stung by the arrow of longing will find high country and virgin land, refuge and solitude nevertheless!

p.38,#73 *Virtus repulsae nescia sordi dae.*[1] In the purity of wish: the widest trajectory. The purer your wish, the less—friction!

p.38,#74 **The misery of publicity.** Where was the driving force of the fiery sting—of coolest possession's discovery! What was land, home—the coolness of the untrodden? The less pretense to publicity you are burdened with, the greater are the possibilities to become an influence in the great depths of the world.

p.40,#77 In the clear will of a *pro domo*[2] (openness—closedness, for all and for no one) lies enclosed the canon of the highest culture experience. An indelibility, a light that defies every storm, is the one—extinguished in home.

To pull the world toward you—by keeping it at a distance: this "attitude of life" was basically always that of art. But this should only be seen as a paradigm! The artistic solitude is a solitude where there is no room for self-sufficiency. Its real lovers have their love, their courage from an economy and a law and pride concealed to the weak ones.

One should never doubt the richness of humankind but certainly its—sincerity: the infallible net to entrap honor and life.

[1] Valour that rejects humiliating repudiation. (Horace)
[2] For one's house—one's own cause.

When you have thrown pedantry overboard, only then does it be- p.41,#79
come a necessity—to be meticulous.

Slowness and sun—the two defenses of old age. A world of hope— p.42
of calm and gentle absurdity—without presumptuousness and spite:
such rhythm and such light may well be the true characteristics of old
age.
    He who knows something about a certain type of fever—gets his
own view of slowness! There were times, when I envied those who
were having a "dull" time.

There is never much in the so-called higher strata that is suited to fill p.43,#85
one's mind with joy, with trust, with a joyous firmness. The isolation
that consists in following one's basic principles will always have its
spontaneous sanction in itself—at least as long as the world looks
the way it does! Surely you have to take care of your eye! The human bootlicker mentality may be a harmless thing—it is not until it
reaches the level of intellectual clarity, yes, the stratum of genius,
that it unfolds its overwhelming stinking power. I believe that Schopenhauer at some point had to hold his—nose when he thought of
Goethe. He did not have to fear the eye.

"The night of the poet."[1] The more profoundly you take the con- p.44,#87
cept of density, the richer your movement, the more victorious the
fending off of the asphyxiating power. "The night of the poet" does
not reach deep enough, is too youthful, too light; is in reality—inclined not to distrust! Voluntariness is a force for which no sacrifice
may seem too great. Only he who has committed himself shall experience the full bliss of an *indulgere genio*.[2] The enticement of what is
difficult lies in the fact that it makes life easy to carry, lightens the
pressure of passions. For those shallow by nature, the talk of art's
austerity is rubbish—a turgid jumble of words.

Legend has a deep sense for clues as to the concept "disinterested." p.46,#89
The productive pivot of clearly envisioned human predicament appears: as opposed to sterile and learned—"idealism." In general, if

[1]By C. J. L. Almqvist, 19th century author.
[2]Sacrifice to one's genius (Perseus).

the purpose is to learn something about human power resources—
then legend is a mine.

The noblest literature is always that most fervently overlooked.
Quite naturally! It belongs exactly to the sorcery of what is close and
simple—its "fabulousness" . . .

p.46,#90 The life interpreting attempt in the legend is always founded on a
strong sense of measure.

"Timing" is the gem of the dead. In the nontime of death, death's
lack of timing, they "live."

p.47,#93 Whole, confident, unassailable: only when you have never taken
credit for a virtue, a praise: "assuredness." Whoever fully dedicated
himself to hope, movement, future, fears more than anything to
succeed.

p.48,#95 "With a corpse in the cargo"[1] . . . In the men of vast concept
such a world of suspicion is certainly not born out of, nor growing
primarily from, any such concern for the fate of the world and
"world culture." I believe that frequently underneath there has been
a professional secret of the most perilous and spiritual kind, by
which they have astounded the world . . . and outsmarted themselves.

p.49,#96 A certain childishness in relation to the healing realities, the spiritual
freedom, space, and purity as the great adventurous allure of the
will to go on living, supersedes by its simple force all instinct of en-
noblement and dignity. Where such cunning has left traces in human history, there is something capable of titillating the desire for
thought and questioning at the core of the human instinct for amazement—even in someone who got tired of enjoying most things
that people regard as astounding.

p.49,#97 A human achievement of bright excellence is still a deed of darkness:
as seen from the dark of the human heart. A person can only take
himself in earnest on the basis of human poverty. Decisiveness in re-

[1]From Ibsen.

gard to confinement, lowliness, school (*schole*)—could turn into happiness personified. Where a human being has lost his poorness lies his true *incipit tragoedia*.[1] But in every deep comprehension of human destitution lies also an *aei d'en stephanoisin*.[2]

Getting ease out of disease: is that not to be—human! p.51,#100
Where would we have protection against wrath if this notion were not allowed to bring light—if the resource of this illumination was not available to us!

What do we really call "clarity?" For the most part a kind of desire for p.51,#101 vengeance; an urge to revenge existence.

Growth is only to be found in a state of austere unpretentiousness. p.79,#50 Without fail, elementary protective powers include spiritual correspondences. There is a life of the eye, which strikes back at any attack as sure as anything else. To live for the freedom of one's eye, the strengthening of the skin of one's soul, is certainty of expansion.

The living light protects, the living light—hides. The whole artistic p.80,#51 character of the aphorism, its *festivum*,[3] lies in its openness—tightness, its character of said—unsaid—"sounding silence."
Antiquity is future. To the extent that the aphorism has been antiquity's mode of thought, it is also the future's. It expresses the "catholic" ideal—without a native country—by means of its openness, lacking shores: the limitless onwards, contained in all pure, human moderation.

There was a largo in Emerson that the Prussian instincts of p.90,#6 Nietzsche revolted against. In what he calls "the undulating" in Goethe, he really encounters the same thing; the human width, the rootedness of a mild culture —the very "southern" character he always had a passion for, and which never revealed itself to him. Against a sense of wisdom (nature of the Muses) he comes flaunting his schooling! Professor's conceit! The impetus of Athenes' grace

[1] The tragedy begins.
[2] (May I dwell) always among those crowned with laurel (Euripides).
[3] Festive joy.

that marked the nobleness of his culture, became Roman brittleness. Did he have too much European Nordicism in his blood to assume the Goethean heritage he seemed worthy of as part of his musical nature?

p.92,#8 A lovely force, which would have built his profound happiness, he wanted to debase into serfdom under crude powers—desire for revenge, where the cause of the inner right of hope had long ago been choked by snobbery, culture quarrel, prancing with words. Music can only be exclusively in the service of adequacy. Anything outside of this (the human *prepon*[1]) is befoulment. It was this crime against music's inner laws that made his world collapse.

p.93,#10 What did Spinoza basically mean by his *amor dei* but the complete dependence upon movement of thought—and the love of this dependence. This in the sense of highest "affect." And in essence this is nothing but what in the language of the mystics is called "weakness," "lowliness," "privation," "hunger."

p.93,#11 It is the inner necessity that is the advantage and the richness. And the final impoverishment of most thinkers (which combines splendidly well with a prolific "productivity") is caused by the substitution of the inner necessity's clear (musical) compulsion by gross (amusical) effects.

p.93,#12 That a *pro domo*[2] is alive, felt as a necessity and something to strive for—is, however, a guarantee eventually experienced by others as a defensive force, as—*pro domo*. It might be a misfortune no longer to be able to feel the enticement of this sting. Its naïve freshness might mean a source of youth, infinitely much more precious than all fame—yes, its upkeep is *eo ipso*[3] continuity, conquest. But only by old age—in rare exceptions—is granted the fusion of evenness and newness that crowns a true life of culture.

p.94,#13 It was the harmony of the search for a climate and for a productive life that brought the rare enchantment of idyll and adventure to

[1]That which suits (a human). (Plato)
[2]For one's house—one's own cause.
[3]Precisely for that reason.

Nietzsche's writings: an *empracticón*[1] leading to the endowment of a perpetual nature's grace, to this whole glimmering movement of wit, of allusion and irony—of Protean life, kynism, and a thinker's bliss. Perhaps there is no better example of asclepiadic reality in recent culture. His engaging powers, his capacity to enthrall, to grip, his most fortunate invention is entirely based upon this foundation.

He will always stand unchallenged, an innovative creator within the Cynicism[2]—searching for clues, in the climactic spirit of exploration. The true fires he lit—those genuinely Genoesan—will not die as long as the human spirit searches for signs and subsistence. p.94,#14

It was possible for him to be able to feel whole and composite, *integer*, only within a very small—a lackluster and "simple" field. This was the new land he really discovered once by Genoesan instinct. To claim it as his—his strength of experience did not suffice: too willingly did he allow himself to be fooled by a European-oriented psychology. p.95,#15

Observe that insofar as the necessity of maintaining a simple independence and unconcern stands clear to him as *rem prorsus substantialem*[3]—he still remains in the dawn of strength, undivided spirit, clear purposes. After he lost this *sub divo*[4]—the cynicism of Inducement—he was exposed to every assault, and his judgment was confused. Yes, has he then not basically (in the same sense as in his own case), in regard to the Greeks, practically always sided with—the disoriented?

How finely he has written—about his own work! Truly, there is more of "*das reinmachende Auge*"[5] in his letters to Overbeck and Peter Gast than in "*Morgenröthe*" itself. At least in relation to his friends he was profoundly and nobly productive. I believe that these letters will survive, indeed have already survived many of his works. His purest desires are expressed through his deep and spiritual concern for need, p.96,#16

[1](Approx.) pragmatism.
[2]From the Greek Kynikos, in the original meaning, emanating from the sect of Greek philosophers founded by Anthistenes, of whom Diogenes was a disciple.
[3]The essential (substantial) matter.
[4]Under the open sky.
[5]The purifying eye.

struggle for dignity, and reverence for life. This fiery spirit fills almost every page of his letters to his friends. The cultural worries that Goethe and Schiller confided to each other in their letters seem cool, almost harmless in comparison. In the *lettere precettive*[1] of humankind (if such a collection were gathered) they would occupy a seat of honor.

p.96,#17   Goethe never became a culture politician. Least of all was he a—"patriot." Anyone who bows to wisdom is not going to be fooled by the time hustle. His whole situation is defined by what Nietzsche once wrote to Peter Gast: "Es gibt keine 'deutsche Kultur' und hat nie eine gegeben, ausser bei mystischen Einsiedlern—*Beethoven und Goethe sehr eingerechnet!*"[2]

p.99,#22   A spiritus rector[3] of Democritus has been a living image to Nietzsche in his first—in reality his single fortunate scope of strategy: "*das reinmachende Auge.*"[4] At this temperature—the rarest of the European spirit—hypnotized by the laws of the human-economic mystery, its fire and its coolness, he encounters the two true masters of later German prose, Lichtenberg and Goethe. Both the *sculptural* and *halcyonic* phases of Nietzsche's history of style are not hard to distinguish, in the light of these educators of his eye, provoking purity of struggle, of lowliness, of joy.

p.99,#23   His instinct turns against the misery of togetherness and ostentatiousness. But the force of his character and experience have proved insufficient for the radical grasping of the fact that you will by no means get at the culture of ostentation by becoming the prey of a higher, a "finer" nature of grandiloquence. Embedded here was a world of wisdom and courage whose brightness his eye shunned, in spite of all his afflictions.

    It is about the character of a human "*prepon,*"[5] in other words, the nature of human energies that all culture tries to provide informa-

---

[1] Representative letters.
[2] "There is no 'German culture' and has never been, except in the case of some lonely mystics—Beethoven and Goethe very much included!"
[3] Guiding spirit.
[4] The purifying eye.
[5] That which suits (a human) (Plato).

tion. No one is more appropriate and better suited than he who has become an outcast by force of conscience and taste. In the case of all energies the grand question is: distance. To have been created for such a life of exploration—having lost the mark of innermost vision—that is to be placed eye to eye with the Medusa of emptiness.

"Aus Koth Gold Machen!"[1] Those words came to Nietzsche in his great p.103,#28
suffering: from Attar, Rumi,[2] and Emerson. But he did not have the musical ear to fathom what "gold" was. And the lightning of truth provided no solace.

Can a person escape from conceit and its shriveling effects with the p.103,#29
aid of a great measure of taste? There are areas in Nietzsche's life and its pathos where such a "moral of the stars" seems waiting to be born.
     What can really be called genuine in a person? Should it be judged according to the degree of calculating wisdom in relation to the finest lures (coolness and "height")? What is most revealing in taste seems to be tied to an economical Jesuitism; to include it among despicable values would be unnatural.

Where all is shell—a dainty, polished shell—one yells: all is—core! p.109,#7

If the only aim of competition is other people's opinion of one's p.112,#13
worth, then one competes simply—for the vapors of others.

Contour is a spice—making other spices superfluous. p.112,#15

Idyl—without élan, without salt: precisely the opposite of idyl. p.113,#16

Where power of experience is lacking, no education, however exten- p.113,#17
sive, helps.

Lowliness is an esthetic-economic, that is, artistic concept, con- p.113,#19
sequently not a sentimental one. It has nothing to do with the "humility" and "unpretentiousness" of contemporaries.

[1]"Turning filth into gold!"
[2]12th century Persian poets.

Where a lasting level of ability to reign has been achieved, there has always been the underlying need for self-conquest. It is questionable if such a feeling can be labeled "purity." In any case, never in a sentimental sense!

For men of thought and taste nothing has ever passed for beautiful except what is of a rough, or in other words, a clean nature! The ethos of sentimentality belongs within the realm of the muddled and the bootlickers, of the Christian—humanistic watery soup—not to the world of taste.

The coarseness of fellowship unfolds best from the point of view of "self-evidence" and "of course" (*hoc est:*[1] the marketing concept) from which they are always basically seen by their courtiers and supporters. Taste is being without a homeland, and no bishop circus. The love of clean air and clean lines is inseparable from a certain misanthropy, a certain—"asocial instinct."

p.116,#24   Against the repugnance of life and the despair of emptiness there is no preventive remedy better than a wisely maintained feeling of gratitude—preserved in the freshness of novelty. And no words speak more surely to my heart than these by the "heathen apostle!": *kathos eleethemen, ouk enkakoumen* (Cor. II, 4).[2] They come from a heart that has tasted weariness—and salvation!

p.116,#25   One ought to be baffled by dullness, but never by—evenness! And how easy it is to confuse the two . . .

p.116,#26   Monotony is something that has to be accepted in its totality! If not, it becomes—"murderous."

The whole, strengthening monotony: life's sweetest wine.

p.117,#27   The thought of unattachment in Plutarch. *Hoi to ta pragmata ton chrematon oneta, me ta chremata ton pragmaton hegeisthai, panton ekratesan*[3]—And being in the lead.

[1]That is.
[2]As we have been endowed with mercy we do not let ourselves be discouraged.
[3]Those who are of the opinion that deeds should be bought with money and that money should not be bought with deeds became masters of all.

Every sun is a sun bypassed. He who is filled with deepest joy is un-disturbed, pragmatic—like the sun; bypassed—like the sun!

Under all circumstances a human being is someone humiliated, passed by—with child and fool in his heart. Would he then not be too proud for—"rightness!" If the unobstructed journey is not reward enough, then there is no reward.

You are not productive . . . but is not this—quiet, youth, novelty! To have had an effect, to "have won approval"—is it not the same as no longer being allowed to feel the eye's profound bliss before an un-restrained field of vision, an untrodden land?

> *Sei nur nicht gemein:*   p.118,#28
> *so kannst du überall in einer Wüste sein.* [1]

That is the only wasteland—the only solitude of value!

Frei, aber Allein . . .[2] Many have known those words! And believed p.118,#29
themselves belonging to the people of light, of pride—but then got
caught in a worse thicket than any hustler of the marketplace.

Searching for the happiness (not "the philosophy") of clear con- p.118,#31
cepts; to look for them—for the sake of the enemies one carries
within oneself—this makes the philosopher.

Loneliness and work's pride. The defensive power of the most subtle, p.119,#32
the elite (according to the Cynics[3]), grows precisely from the common things. Regimen, order—natural means of isolation! Whoever
loves the rule, will love the burden—yes, will put his whole life at
stake for this love. Without everyday's fire of joy to him all will be—
loneliness.

To kairon[4] a state of equilibrium between inexhaustible elements of p.121,#37
soundness and a limitless store of what leads up to them (causti-
cum). Freedom: close, within touch! But nearness always blinds.

[1]"Only don't be base
  and you'll be at home in a desert, any place."
[2]Free, but alone . . .
[3]From the Greek *Kynikos* in the original meaning.
[4]The right moment.

Where nearness and distance become one is the living fulcrum. A "vaticinium"[1] of something great is always founded on something inexhaustibly delicate, burning. *Tu Marcellus eris . . .*[2]

Even the bliss of the "probable foundation"—from here seen as something inferior! Authenticity as the foundation of bliss—the certainty of being chosen for experience on account of a "virus"; congruency's sensation as apparition (*Themata—Chremata!*)[3] granting sudden solace by a certainty of infiniteness, unobstructedness . . .

p.122,#39 The genesis of steel, its "idiosyncracy"? The same divination of character on his own behalf, which brought about Goethe's interpretation of Frederick the Great, comes forth in Nietzsche, in his way of looking at Demosthenes. The difference lies in the fact that Goethe feels himself to be a superior power, who—obeys. His thought of submission is anchored in non-violent thought; his will to power is a will to music. To lead and rule mightily is his passion, and yet this urge did not harm his soul because out of this passion rose another: that of his stalking sense, his heuristics; his love of being led and governed by that which is softest.

p.123,#41 "Do not envy yourself": Dante's great words—the simple expression of salvation's thought. Not to let clandestine purposes and calculations steal your strength. In freedom from planning and calculation: led and conducted. Does one really possess one's **why** except when one is—**the farthest out?** Where one has no other enemy but oneself: where one does not accuse. Unswerving spirit and immaculate journey—traveling high, without pride's agony and shamefulness.

The danger of confusion, of being directed away from his great nature, lurked much closer to Dante than to Goethe. Basically he was not a "fighter!" There is fortunately an actual and productive world—hidden by a lack of luster—a world that exists behind the well-documented one. No one has a better advantage than he who by the force of his vision has been given a lodestar in a true titanic spirit's possibility of salvation and homecoming: he who by the force of such vision, such timeliness—is "untimely."

[1]Prediction, prophesy.
[2]You shall be (a new) Marcellus (Virgil).
[3]My themes, my property!

Picciola.[1] Where human lowliness has been encountered—around p.124,#42 such a place there will be growth and flourishing! No doubt, it is indicative of something human, and deeply informative about the mystery of human possession that emerges in the fact that a work such as **Picciola** has had the profound and refined success it once had and still quietly has; that it has been appealing, stimulating, soothingly cooling to so many humanly full-blooded personalities. This is because the episode that is its real essence (the prisoner and the plant) is based upon the elementary, inexhaustible truth, and points at a strong strain of law. Its secret presence constitutes the power of spell and music of sirens underneath this poetry—so beyond all poetic conventionality. **Nothing** lies deeper embedded in the heart of adventure and its murmur of wind than what is home to a human being. There is no void more glaring on the map of human explorations than that of human happiness! Power radiates where a human heart has been hidden—hidden, as only a human heart can be, in what is close.

Those who have expressed the richness of what is close—you will p.125,#44 never meet them among the myopically wise, never among those closed in by greed.

Nietzsche and Spinoza. In limitation's coolness he encountered p.125,#45 him—and at that moment he felt like an explorer of space and trajectory—finding a possibility of expansion in this limitation—that suddenly cascaded the Genoese purple of a goodby over this encounter!

The most important information has often sprung from the source p.128,#53 and the circumstances of never having taken good news seriously!

"The thorn-strewn path of honor" was lovely to tread for many—as p.129,#55 compared with that which started when honor had been achieved! Ola Hansson[2] complains that he finds his situation in later days more difficult, far more difficult—after he had been recognized, than during the times of complete silence and lack of understanding. What does this mean? That he took recognition in earnest! Had this not

[1]Work by X. Boniface Saintine.
[2]Early 20th century Swedish poet.

been the case, he would still have felt himself as being part of strife and youth, as being in the heart-strengthening, will-soaring, incomprehensibility's youth and its boldness. You are not siding with soundness until you realize and feel joy at the insight that one should fear recognition more than despair. Such insight will never lead to public acclaim.

p.132,#59   *Phoibos*[1]—purest string of gold: inducement's stability and density. Firm ground and being in the lead is nothing but a youthful relation to inducement and inducement's density: precisely the circumstances, the lack of which "youth" (in the word's petty, empty meaning) suffers and has to suffer.

keio d'hos to paros per aupnous nyktas iauon[2]

There you have culture's adventure and . . . culture's conscience! The principle of salt and of movement. It is this peacefulness—spark and a reserve fund—this fastidiousness and this contempt (*filoponou psyches*)[3] that you must wake up to each day. What is all fullness of life, all lustre, as compared to being worthy of such poorness, such—stronghold!

p.133,#62   *In den Alpen bin ich unbesiegbar, namentlich wenn ich allein bin und ich keinen andern Feind als mich selber habe.*[4] Yes, this is the paradigm for this kind of man. Either these "alps"—or nothing. And still he has to create for himself another land of alps, a second light, precisely— "the light of the alps" in the midst of this either-or! With a certain bitterness one has kept quiet about this—kept quiet, asked, waited.

p.134,#63   The relation to cynicism[5] in Emerson as well as in Nietzsche was the best clue I could wish for. Certainly, this was nothing else but the "Rousseauism"—authenticity and happiness—that out of experience and studies I had realized long before. "Medicine and physiology—in reality my lodestars!" says Nietzsche. And for what other reason would we have anything to do with Nietzsche . . . But it is

[1]Phoebus—Apollo, the sun god.
[2]I want to sleep as before I lay sleepless at night. (The Odyssey)
[3]With a work-loving soul.
[4]When I am in the alps I am invincible, that is, when I am alone and have no other foe but myself (Nietzsche, 1877).
[5]From the Greek *Kynikos*.

precisely the way he let this sound eye be dimmed, this entirely sound aristocracy be exchanged for the vulgar happiness of fighting and its *amusi*[1]—this constitutes one of the finest values of explicitness I have encountered in the history of culture.

If you meet what you are supposed to meet in the purest sense, the p.141,#2 world will eventually meet you.

The care, pain, and doubt of character will be balanced there. Life's result does not lie in width or expanse, it may lie in instants. And what has been postponed by reason of road and effort is well postponed. In Vain can be the greatest gain. Perhaps it is the great human In Vain that the wisest ones have taught their souls to sacredly revere—for the joy of the road!

There is a yielding to the conditions of one's own character that leads to the most joyous courage, and opens the way to one's best possibilities. The eye of the unbending hides many a slyness, cunning . . . and shrewdness.

And in your self-reproach do not forget the bitterly honest notion, honest contempt of the bootlicker world that filled and captured your mind from your earliest years! Do justice to yourself! Perhaps there is a suffering baptized by reason, a separating archetype, without which you would never have tasted the joyous light of courage! The intensity of the first lights—the first flames of anger at the violation of taste and pride . . . Perhaps this very spark from the depths of the dark passions (if this region could be kept clean to your eye!) may give purpose and wholeness to your journey; perhaps even the hope of belonging with those who bravely, clearly turned themselves against their own hearts' treachery and darkness; who were not silenced, and did not give in to the stings of pain caused by the imbalance between the superficial world and inexorable longing's demand, forcing fountains of hope to burst forth—so that their names could be erased from the list of traitors to the idea!

The untouched, beauty in its wild state: is nothing but the economy p.142,#4 of your natural distance relation. How often do you see that the illusion of togetherness, with all its concessions to taste by half-mea-

[1]Amusia = something amusical.

sures, has given rise to the most dangerous of inner disorders. *Nulla via celerior est ad insaniam quam ira.*[1]

Life in the service of truth, beauty, and exploration has no other lodestar than the deep jealousy of truth and beauty! They yield themselves only to whoever surrenders to them—as to a rescuer.

The warmth that can make something crooked become straight, something wrongful harmless to your reason, is only achieved by the No which extinguishes all wrath, all anger, all repentance. *Nulla via celerior est ad beatitudinem quam abnegatio sui ipsius!*[2]

p.143,#5 *Cantabit vacuus . . .*[3] The words of those incurably supersensitive, who have tried to find their salvation and escape in the sweetness and triumph of the dark eye, the foresight, and the power of anticipation!

p.145,#9 "Your lamp bore a quite different witness!" exclaimed Demosthenes. This is the very question. Where is the borderline between ideas and the prosperous market! Where one has searched for something "higher" it sometimes seems as though the intention had been to make for oneself something lower, treacherously dispensable—as if one had strived for something (noncompetitive!) higher—insidious?

p.145,#10 It is wondrous—that honor and life, and richness of thought have been granted to a human being with such reasonable conditions as a preserved clarity of image of a genuine, purely desired, and disinterested condition; only as little as a grain of additional weight on the side of the disinterested will is capable of causing an intensified breath of humanism (spirit and freedom).

Antiquity: the thought of unattachment—the grand human line, and innermost pride and joy's politics that have revealed themselves to me in glimpses from mysticism's vision experience, from poorness and "emptiness," as the abstention I had to approach and try to penetrate, and find: on one side, clarity about the nature of victory—

[1] No road leads faster to insanity than wrath (Seneca).
[2] No road leads faster to bliss than self-denial.
[3] Cantabit vacuus (coram latrone viator): The penniless traveler will sing in the presence of the highwayman; i.e., the penniless man has nothing to lose (Juvenal).

and on the other side, a pure concept of contempt. Where could I obtain a better reason for my power of literary research as well as my empathy, "philology," as well as for my strongest inner life as an author!

The first lights are decisive. A love for studies built on an observance p.168,#33 of deeply simple, childishly serious conditions may do miracles. Not only Swedenborgian experiences and awakenings might grant the right to "associate with spirits." He who reached into the deep significance of the concept school (although surrounded by a world of high-flown "culture") may form alliances and receive information never dreamed of by the highbrow learned. In this respect at least I have been honest, been real. Empty studies, empty names never existed for me. To me all was thirst for communion, a fear of isolation—blood—thirst.

Whoever by his nature is predestined for freedom, there is for him p.169,#34 really no development. *Omnia sua secum*[1]: his whole development lies in a first light, a beginning, an earliness.

The greatest value an author can convey to me seems to consist in p.170,#2 some mysterious spice—by the power of which he becomes insufficient to me . . .

[1](Carries) with him all (that is) his.

Plus Salis / 1945

p.10,#14 It is by no means certain that the common sense of the Chinese strikes home as far as their sense of community is concerned:

"Virtue is not left to stand alone, he who practises it will have neighbours" (Confucius).[1]

That might just as well be a philistine sentence—sly and saturated with blood thirst. How many a dragon has not been hatched in the marshland of "loving kindness," the swamp of community!

Every reasonable human being—as a separate individual—must understand that war is a stupidity. As soon as he is in "his element," namely in the mass, at once he understands something else: that in the end stupidity is the right thing! Ergo: long live the collective. Cursed be all uniqueness!

What is it that makes war possible—if not servility! War is the triumph of common servility. A tempest of servility.

p.12,#17 Nobody will experience a more derogatory and bitter loneliness than he who is rejected by solitude.

Solitude is a deity and requires faith—and an altar built anew every day.

Its probable foundation lies entirely in the regimen of care one can muster for solitude.

[1]From Legge (Author's note).

There are people never capable of telling a lie. There is simply no p.13,#19
room for a lie in them: their whole nature is a lie!

That all is in vain, does that mean then that all is futile? It could mean p.15,#24
the very opposite! It was the mystery of the virtus-thought, of possessing it, that once and for all became essential to man. The profound gentlemen who found that man is small—because the uni-
verse is so very big . . . no use wasting any words on them.

The innermost shrine of all our knowledge—and the most indis- p.15,#25
pensable of all—is in fact always that which is of no use!
   Real strength and unfailing joy exist only when you have reconciled yourself to the thought of losing everything. If everything in
this world were not in vain, what would then be of interest!

Instants only! Perhaps . . . but instants that could leave never-ending p.15,#26
wells in our consciousness.
   Where there is no other ownership but through art and thought—
there the moments will be found, the most vital, most essential to us,
those that if overlooked, would leave everything rich and beautiful a
poisonous sting, a cruel mockery.

Out of plain air they seem to have taken them, literally—their p.57,#39
strongest powers of balance. So with Landor and Emerson, so with
Whitman and Nietzsche: by instinctive force of ancient culture (total
concurrence of nature and profound knowledge)—pragmatic poetry, pragmatic wisdom. As soon as this divination of an archaic and
healing life ideal had flared up, they were filled with a fruitful possibility of continuation. Days of happiness . . . days—when they felt as
though a single hour of pure blissful insight—on a shore, in the
woods, had advanced them, brought them further than months of
study!

Meden agan.[1] p.66,#10
   Without any question the *metron* doctrine—that is: the doctrine
of Enough—coincides with the Indian-Chinese teachings of a fully

[1] Not too much.

realized way of breathing as the source of the perpetuation of thought, the principle of hope and belief: *entelēcheia*.[1]

(To be seized by Enough: to be seized by the eternity thought.)

p.67,#11 The boundary is the meeting place—the meeting the border. *Hora vivendi*[2] occurs and stands firm when the insight of this concurrence, its need to be the first and the most essential, has become all-fulfilling, all-encompassing, all-illuminating.

As compared to the great happening of this stoic *Nunc*[3]—which really isn't, cannot be anything but the event of Mysticism—what pitiful obscurity is then all we call clarity, harmony, atticism, wisdom, and many other beautiful things in a Montaigne. How ardently has Pascal rejected all this!

p.69,#15 "Asklepieion"—Experience: *he ariste mousike*.[4] And that was my course. From "metron-theme" through "bow and lyre world"—to Experience. I started my most substantial work as an author late in life. I had barely guessed at the wellspring of experience-power and wholeness, even less tasted it, as I approached my forties.

p.72,#1 The difficult efforts are not involved in intellectual, but in emotional work. It is not for the sake of happiness we look for the clear concepts: neither because of the enemies we harbor within us—but for the sake of those who envy us, our adversaries.

It is precisely by personally taking matters in earnest, "matter-of-factly," that you free yourself from the titanic efforts! You are never without defense against stupidity until you have become defenseless against your own indignation.

One has never really triumphed over one's enemies except in one way: by having no time for them!

p.79,#12 The more one gives in to hatred, to revenge, to indignation—the more defiant, the more "productive" one's diligence!

But whoever had the feeling that his innermost, most holy protec-

---

[1]Continuation.
[2]The hour to live (Horace).
[3]Now.
[4]The best music.

tion and citadel lay in art's defiance—he fears worse than death the denial of defiance.

"*Nil desperandum!*"[1] Perhaps there still is a "royal road to philosophy?" Maybe it is called the true pride and joy of the eye. Because the divine is simple.

Mysticism is clarity and enigma. There is nothing enigmatic about the obscure.

"*Nil desperandum!*" What is this "clarity" then? Is it not a kind of—music! But isn't philosophy itself the best music?

The vulgarly titanic (the brilliantly titanic) remains one of my most fruitful observations. An attempt at a culture critique that certainly is not on a small scale! p.80,#13

My point of cultural polemics is the experience that is: Plato, Music, Bow-and-Lyre.

That which is most lasting and durable in a human being often evolves from something grossly neglected: it so often has the character of something recaptured. Many a mistake wakens the spirit of youth, of conquest—so much power that enriches, gives birth to ideals, and draws its most valued nourishment, its rarest élan from the feeling of vindictiveness and rapacity toward the past and its humiliations! From there it is but a short step to the concept of the human as one great abomination—and from there we are also close to hope and enthusiasm's incessantly defiant: p.81,#1

kalos tes tyches hegoumenes[2]

The human predicament is poverty: the fundamental viewpoint of mysticism. And mysticism is nothing but economy—a pragmatic, living, productive economy. How should I prepare for myself the densest, strongest net for catching life? Mysticism's eternal question and concern. All these economists—*oikonomoi mysterion theou*[3]—are jealous of hunger, of poverty. Only from there will you comprehend what to them is the truth of life and their fitness to live. p.86,#1

[1]One should not despair.
[2]When fate leads graciously.
[3]Guardian of God's secrets (Paul).

and so we'll live
and take upon the mysteries of things,
as if we were God's spies.

Yes, and this is the very place where he is at home: the one overflowing with life—Shakespeare!

p.87,#3 Tempest and *euphemia*[1]: the formula of the aesthetic paradox!
Really, to Plato, Michelangelo, and Shakespeare this was no "Attic,"
no "aesthetic" experience . . .

No, an experience of the divine: the mystery of the virtus-
thought. The life struggle was ultimately about its capture.

p.87,#4 Shakespeare and the spirit's care of nourishing—*a pulcrum et prae-
clarum quod sua sponte peteretur*[2]: that is a viewpoint from which one
could approach the so-called "sonnet problem." **Being struck by
the thought** and the question of a disinterested search, knowledge,
and love-devotion's possibility in man—therein lies the meeting
ground, the mystery that linked together the greatest ones, those
aflame, those alive. Thus, even some of those "strange poems"
might be seen as Shakespeare's most profound confession, his true
history.

p.89,#2 *Psyches ananke*[3]: Sublime discipline and—entrustment. Where Plato
reveals himself as a Pythagorean, where Goethe eventually had to
meet Kant: search there!

I do not think that one can advance any further into Platonism
than with the aid of Plato's own sources, those that have determined
his innermost critique: those Pythagorean-Orphic ones, those of the
muses. Such a Platonism unravels in Goethe's last great phase of development.

p.90,#3 State: position—pose. Spirit versus state! Perhaps Kierkegaard is
one of the few to maintain a clear line here. And the key to Plato's
character, which has been the object of so much searching, could it
be found in the Platonic—**breach of faith?**

[1]Eloquent by virtue of being taciturn.
[2](Something) beautiful and excellent sought after for its own sake.
[3]Insistence of the soul.

The East's great corrective of all titanic intellectualism, all fake culture, and excessive learning, is breathing brought to perfection. Tao is such an orientation. Maybe Socrates was as anticultural as Lao-tse, more inclined toward the East than Plato. What can we really know about Socrates? Plato is actually the one who armed Socrates; in other words: gave him the weapons he—Plato—needed.

Could Socrates have entertained thoughts of radicalism, for which Plato was not daring enough (you always suspect traces of a decorum, of a Western orientation, in the latter)? Is Socrates not a misanthrope!

How a person grows: Could that mean anything but how a human p.90,#4
becomes what "human" means—one who measures! When an Augustine and a Dante are set on fire in the same flame by one word—what does that mean? The basis of the virtus concept could prove to be like the Solon-heritage: metrics! Is it in the art of measuring (how does one become worthy of one's thought, worthy of what one says!) that a human's full and real history and growth lies?

All sublime curiosity centers on the mystery of human ownership p.92,#8
(the acquisition of reality): *aliquid natura pulcrum quod sua sponte peteretur.*[1] It is here that the music, in the Platonic sense enlightenment's piece of art in the human soul, has to prove itself. It is obvious that only by focusing on the enigma that for Plato hides underneath *arete* (virtus),[2] one may perceive his unsentimental concept of the urge for acquisition of knowledge.

Maybe some of the brightest words, worthy of a *misólogos*,[3] that ever p.92,#9
flowed from Goethe's pen—are these about Winckelmann:

> *Aber er hatte etwas aus den Alten gewonnen, was die
> Philologen von der Gilde gewöhnlich zuletzt oder gar
> nicht lernen, weil es sich nicht aus, sondern an ihnen
> lernen lässt—ihren Geist . . .*[4]

[1] Something naturally beautiful sought for its own sake.
[2] Virtue.
[3] Misologist.
[4] But he has won something from the ancient which those who belong to the fellowship of the Philologists generally learn last or not at all, because it cannot be learned from them but of them—their spirit . . .

That may be—yet, I sometimes blasphemously wonder about this lighthearted credulity: that this misology, this cultural skepticism, did not reach any further! How childishly bright he stands out if placed next to one of those with a really sharp eye, a *dysgoeteutos*,[1] a Plato!

p.99,#10 War is a vast incomplexity.

Being able to tell those insipid people the truth about their barrenness, this you can only achieve as the ideal wanderer—Asclepiadic, gymnastic, pragmatic: like a man who has no other enemies but himself!

Where you dwell in order to meet your thought—"Egeria"[2]—only there are you freed from the ever plebeian triviality of a criticism that has no other inspiration than the inability to "let others live,"—the desire to declare one another redundant!

p.100,#12 Taste is truly a moral reality!

"*Denn ich entsprang . . .*"[3] Nietzsche was full of joy the day he uttered those words: still happier the day he—lived them.

p.100,#13 "*Denn ich entsprang!*"—may be the most joyous sentence in Nietzsche's whole work. Thus, there lay a more treacherous snare before him than that of the "Christian ideal!"

"*Procul dubio!*"[4] It was the "nationalism" in Richard Wagner that disgusted Nietzsche. He was disappointed in him as a true despiser— a *désintéressé*—not to mention his—"entourage!"

"*Denn ich entsprang!*" *L'homme sans prises!* The man without thought of attachment—*solutus omni foenore.*[5] Truly rich and happy is only he for whom this question of climate, this "bohême," this lack of a homeland has become the conscience and sum of all questions!

[1]The one who is difficult to seduce.
[2]In Roman mythology, a nymph who acted as adviser and dictated laws to Numa, second king of Rome.
[3]"Thus I escaped . . ."
[4]"Far from doubt!"
[5]L'homme sans prises (someone who has managed to keep away from capture): solutus omni foenore (Author's note).

*alla to me labein kreitton kai periousia tes aretes, en hois
exestin, epideiknymenes to me deomenon.*
(Plutarch: Aemilius Paulus)[1]

The only way to get at the fake culture and the togetherness sham, is p.101,#14
to deliver oneself to the thought of art, along the road of true mysticism. What a gem: the manly insatiable, unaspiring spirit—its scorn
and contempt, its hunger!

How moments could glow even for a Keller, when the meaning of
the Goethean abnegation—as a basic condition for highest art, composure, maturity, a sharp eye—seemed fully grasped and consummated! How a human life—with all of its dull and sluggish length—
is nevertheless insufficient!

The human thought—"thoughts wandered": thus the road (not the p.103,#16
goal) is the positive, the ultimate.

The quintessence of Lessing's thought is this:

The world of truth is no place for us. Only on our way do we
breathe. Apollo: always the God of the way, always—aguieus![2]

It is as if the result, the victory disarmed one . . . The one rendered
powerless, that is—you!

Combattre toute ma vie![3]

Finally, here lies the radical turnabout, the reevaluation: the
changed perception. The Necessity that is the opposite of everything
convulsive.

Bring this with you everywhere, this bright war! And that other
war won't bog you down in its swamp, won't suffocate you.

It is precisely this which is the essence and the content—the liber- p.103,#17
ating and sublime in all that is tone: that there is no "why!" no "to
what avail!"

There is only one way to compete, but—the greatest one: free voli- p.108,#25
tion!

Those anxious to acquire knowledge, experience, have all been

---

[1]It is preferable not to accept (rewards) and it is the essence of virtue to be found demanding nothing, even where reward is due.
[2]God of the way!
[3]Contend all my life!

marked by the stamp of the fugitive: Fear of avarice, terror, and disgust at the whole bootlicker world.

Quid licet Jovi non bovi.[1] But—with all the grateful piety for Walter Scott left in me from childhood—I must admit that Beethoven is right a thousand times when throwing Walter Scott's book onto the floor with a furious: *"der Kerl schreibt ja doch nur für Geld!"*[2]

p.110,#30   *Patiens-vigil*[3]: to will . . . and not to will. What does Orpheus signify? That will to power is will to music. Only the one with the cool hands shall lift the treasure. All things draw close to whoever shelters the right music.

Perhaps the Orpheus myth is the Greek myth *"par excellence"*?[4] There is a Faustean theme that runs through all peoples whose culture has had a lasting influence on humanity. The Greeks searched for the solution in music.

The most precious truths are those that befall man as if at play, as *musicus*. The play is the basic activity. The play: the great economy. *"Man muss dem Schicksal nicht merken lassen, was man will."*[5] Yes, at that time he was on the road of quietism! Of quietism: of the human economy.

p.113,#34   Those who have offered sound coins, clearly marked—they were no "easy marks": those who found no other honor worthy of their dream, but that which results from being used by everyone and thanked by no one—being disregarded like the sun: they are to be envied; they are those who have been fortunate in the art of thinking, in poetry.

Their entire art of living (cunning wisdom and politics!): wanting to be the **magnetic force** of certain questions, certain things.

p.115,#3   Pindar, the Edda, yes, even the Old Testament point clearly to the fact that if there is—interplay (life interplay!)—the "logical" relationship often may prove to be precisely—its opposite.

[1] That which Jupiter is allowed is not permissible for the beast of burden.
[2] "but the fellow writes only for money!"
[3] Patient-watchful.
[4] of preference.
[5] One should not give fate the opportunity to know what one wants (Nietzche).

The aphorism: the pragmatic literary form *par excellence*. Wander- p.115,#4
er's thought—contrary to paid thought.

In the encounter and the happening *solutus omni foenore*.¹ Here is
demarcation—(*to aphorismēnon*).²

The fullness of the moment and its definition *"Ein würdiger Einschnitt in Zeit und Ewigkeit."*³

Exactly by means of the characteristics: density, compression, p.115,#5
weight (all that the Greeks called *drimytes*)⁴ you may avoid appearing
strained! Whether you will succeed in saying a word of wisdom, of
grace, of—lightness, depends precisely upon possessing that quality.

Sentence plainspoken—and contrary to the learned variant! From p.118,#12
it springs the "good expression's" secret of art, its openness, its freedom of homeland; the invariable actuality of this philological-philo-
sophical experience, the *diánoia*⁵ of true humanism, its real program
and vision! This is realized to the utmost degree of lucidity: a most at-
tentive suitability for the free play of inclination toward clarity, for
the refinement of power of expression and accuracy, calling forth
physically, asclepiadically active conditions—through favorable or
unfavorable circumstances bringing forth a deeply joyous concentration of thought and life activity. Such forces compel one to obey
them and use them as nature's hint and preparation, the clue to the
clearest observation, and inclination, an urge for research!

Seen in the right perspective, I guess I have to recognize that Lichten- p.119,#13
berg's grasp of life seems to be vaster than that of Lessing. Where—if
at all—can one talk about a wide range of understanding for life, if
not in the writings of those who thought on their own behalf and not
at all on account of "humanity"! Lichtenberg was a professor at a university, but his character as an original thinker was not limited by this
fact. In reality, Lessing is much closer to the professor-of-philosophy
type.

Invaluable is Schopenhauer's opinion of Lichtenberg! His most

¹Free of all gain (Horace).
²That which is demarcated.
³A worthy nick in time and eternity.
⁴Roughness, acerbity.
⁵(Animus) State of mind.

powerful (most discrete!) inner sphere cannot be better outlined to one's eye than by looking at it in the light of his deep feeling of friendship for Lichtenberg.

p.120,#14 The tension, the oneness, life interplay: precisely by virtue of the anciently pragmatic, the prehistorically unmethodic!

Thus one might say that an Emerson does not approach the meeting of his fate[1] with a clear grasp of an extreme and fertile situation, that thus "a philosopher in him is lost." And definitely not in Nietzsche's sense!

Because it is here, precisely where he took the fatal step away from his course, as well as nature, and thus lost his protective shield, the asclepiadic, self-healing power of the Muses, which was the major capital of his ingenuity.

The soundness of the moment is this: "Don't turn back!"— and all the spiritual fire of youth has breathed these words of a magic tale. Here is the true moment of "Egeria." The Love Encounter, the meeting with Numa.[2] When Nietzsche steps beyond himself and his protective defense, and becomes a "theoretician," an intention thinker, a calculation thinker—he is rendered skinless. Living thought needs another atmosphere, another tone (another silence!) than that of the dead calculus. There is no need to protect what is dead.

Now his innermost organs gasp for air—the fertile cool atmosphere of honest human poverty, human lowliness! "Please see to it now that I may go into hiding again . . ."

Please give me back now my humble connection with life—the holy poverty and power of true purpose!

p.121,#15 Would one be ready for the discovery that Nietzsche's creative element is to be found in his pure aphoristics? That his "science" ranks only second—and not even that! Because between the two lies his— by no means ordinary—poetry.

Just as there was a land and a field where Hamann and Lichtenberg were at home, the choicest one in common for them both, and

[1] *apoleiphthenai kai ou paraschein hauton* (Isocrates) (keep away, making oneself unavailable) (Author's note).
[2] Mythical Roman king who loved the nymph Egeria (Plutarch).

where he too had domiciliary rights, more so than most people, just as surely the light from this Nietzschean land will one day find its admirers.

He who knows that he has very little to say is likely to become long-winded. Not until he is filled to overflowing does he become artistic, laconic, lapidary, he becomes filled to overflowing. p.121,#16

Openness: only by density. The open words: by the density of continuous inner life. Between speaking and keeping quiet lies a world of its own: the great world of confession—art.[1]

Plato's misology: the line of lines! —The metron that leads on. p.122,#17

That is the only real width that any culture concept has had the power to fathom: Promethean shore, Helichrysan field, the *aphorismēnon*[2] which never was anything but "*das reinmachende Auge.*"[3]

The thought of the Greek Muses—as a bridge to the real European culture: the Music, which is the true escape to nature, the escape from—music! The Music for which Nietzsche once lit fires of joy—in the names of Emerson, Spinoza and Goethe—the joy of experiencing, for the first time, true classicism.

Di bene fecerunt[4]: to be able to express these words, of the aristocratic, the artistic frugality of true—width! p.123,#18

To have one's day fulfilled and to be sustained by this morale: like someone entitled to a great source of nourishment, to great diligence!

Where would the real width of an author show, if not in the art of hitting—the smallest possible target!

Geijer[5] was probably as poor an authority on Homer as Walter

---

[1]The aphorism belongs entirely within the realm of art. Sundbärg, the lauded Swedish "aphorist," was an artless man—a thoroughly leather-like Swedish brain. There is not one aphorism in his famous book. If there had been only a dozen, that would have been enough to chase away his readers (Author's note).
[2]That which is demarcated.
[3]The purifying eye.
[4]The gods did well.
[5]19th century Swedish poet.

Scott, in whom he finds a kinship with Homer—because of Scott's famous "epic" nature, "width," etc. —No art aims at any width, least of all the Homeric.[1]

p.123,#19 The discipline: to be able to say: *Di bene fecerunt*[2]—to own in these words one's criterion of knowledge and being—for art, home.

The means: the coolness and freedom, "the egotistic attitude . . ." *fieri suum*.[3]

Fieri suum (to be given back to yourself): the asclepiadic Priority. Precisely—"the iron-hard regimen."

Never to let the struggle deemphasize it and make it a matter of secondary importance.

Nothing can be more pragmatic than the means!

p.124,#20 When all is summed up this is the greatest adventure: to be able to look upon the day as the most outstanding event.

p.124,#21 Those with a real power to perceive, those touched by the light of joy—only in the most tenuous of all fragile things lies their possibility to grasp the great span.

p.144,#5 To encounter one's thought: That it is the means that are the starting point; that the ways and means are power to discover; this is enviably, superbly simple.

In the words of Geijer: "self-generating by means of inner evolution."

"Self-generating": that is—voluntary.

Herein lies the protection against all hustling, politics, lust for power—the world of wrath.

p.146,#8 Sharp-wittedness is not enough, neither is learning nor vocation sufficient: without the affliction called power of experience you are nevertheless someone poor in spirit.

With regard to experience and practical knowledge how gross the

---

[1]Walter Scott's novels have as little in common with the spirit of the Homeric art as Fröding's (19th century Swedish poet) "biblical" recitations have with the Old Testament (Author's note).
[2]The gods did well.
[3]Become one's own.

calculating thinker, the "scholarly philosopher" can be—that is something one hesitates for a long time to make clear to oneself! What grossness there is in such a concept as a "practitioner by reasoning!"

And—God have mercy!—the taste of these "learned men" . . . The proud philosopher . . . if flattered by a mediocre brain—presto! there he is making his bows! And is ready to declare a tramp's frame of mind for idealism. So there they gather—in "unison." He was always very particular about the fact that there could be no tampering with morals, this philosopher! But tampering with taste—would that not be the same as corrupting morals?

You advance and fulfill yourself by following the practical road— p.150,#2
could there be any doubt about that! But how could there ever be a lack of inducement for this explorer's voyage! The futility of all human conditions places this before our eyes. Already in the conditions of our physical awareness there is—an Ariadne-thread laid out! Exactly the simple, the elementary, the asclepiadically low to respond to!

How many people have not at the outset of their journey had a rich, beautiful, disinterested perception of these things. Why are the first lights so rarely heeded? Why is there so seldom youthfulness in study and school: rarely anything but scanty and bitter competition—so seldom a *humanum per se*!

The secret of always feeling young, never suffocated by "the vanity of all," surely lies in a life tempo that builds itself from the revelation of all pretensions' hopelessness. Where people groan incessantly because of the emptiness in all human endeavor, what we hear is in reality the moaning of the insatiable hunger for power, aspirations' disappointment. The sickly sweetness of honor and pretension destroys Innovation. The great life tempo is the true dampener of pretensions—and creator of innovation.

Those profoundly and deeply suspicious: those who have made p.151,#4
themselves independent of suspicion's agony by looking upon man as a "suspect subject"—they have all been burned except those who loved the fire!

p.152,#6 The soundest evenness of aging: from the power to reject something attained, something achieved; to still remain the blank page—for struggle, for spring.

The great art of youthfulness: someone always at the beginning, always able to return to school, to be a gatherer, a worshiper of all beginnings and first lights. To be devastated is not really fearful; to the contrary: the thought of having achieved something is full of fear!

p.152,#7 The characteristic of youth is that theme does not fail it. It is the web.

What characterizes "youth" (in the trivial sense) is exactly being without a focus—without a theme.

Solid ground is the most eloquent. Therefore: *nosce te ipsum.*[1] The clearest naturalism! And you are the happiest when all you need for orientation is a good fighting spirit.

Whoever feels always the necessity of being prepared to answer and be on his guard, for him there is a first and inevitable condition: *esse.*[2]

The answers—can wait!

p.157,#2 No one causes as much irritation as he who goes against the tide— and at the same time maintains his openness and clarity. It is not with satire one challenges the insipid spirit most profoundly!

There is a way to prolong life and give it strength by making the right enemies: drawing the right nourishment from antagonism. On the strength of such a move you might also find something of the cunning and shrewdness at the service of a dominant desire for unconcern and coolness—like a heavy downpour, an intellect's cold shower on your feelings. Thus it was made possible for the human genius to exist at all: to endure the high pressure under which he has to go on living.

p.161,#7 Only taste protects. A genius has never paid heavier dues than when conforming to a mediocre taste.

Those born with gold in their souls will also experience gold's jealousy.

[1] Know yourself.
[2] To be.

To be prepared at any moment to fall back upon one's inner defenses and life's independence! That is the rule and has always been.
This need and this necessity are evidenced by every phase of *their*
lives. Thus: there is nothing more dangerous than whatever im-
pedes, paralyzes this movement! In this respect, allowing oneself to
be lulled into a sense of security, into a "natural carelessness," is to
them precisely—diverging from nature. Here Michelangelo's saying
carries its full weight in all its relentlessness, in all its stern rapture: *E
di quel c'altri muor, convien ch'i' viva.* (What others die from is for me—
to live.)

To tes diaites amikton![1] Once born an old gossip: no wonder you wor- p.162,#9
ship "togetherness . . ."
Without the stuffiness, the phony communion, man in general is
like a fish on land!
In this tepid world of gossip—is it surprising that there are occasions when an honest man would wish—as the highest honor, the
ultimate reward—to incur the hatred of the people! All pertaining
to the concept humanism, from the standpoint of antiquity's idea
of *virtus*, could be summarized by the idea *l'homme rebours*[2]: as it has
been embraced and shaped by Plutarch-dedicated men in France
(long before Rousseau!).
Music and spirit can never be part of an "upper-class" faction of
existence. Even in the freest, coolest, and most profoundly quiescent
of pagan cultures they confirm their alienation from, their animosity
toward the world—yes, one feels tempted to use the word precisely
in its Christian sense!

This profundity of togetherness with all its precious servility full of p.163,#10
disdain, humility, and condemnation—what was then in essence
the aim of all its reproach and all its deep meaning?
In fact, the more stupid and brutish you are, the less reason you
have to fear people! All doors stand open for the bootlicker.
All through life they tread the road of cowardice and publicity's
tailcoating and gossiping. On this noble elevation the taste has rip-

[1] The pure; an unsociable way of life.
[2] Man against the tide.

ened, the criterion unified. Based on the strength of their experience, the only style these men could utilize to preach and explore is the one called the back-slapper-style.

p.165,#12 There have been many kinds of "witch hunts" in this world—that made the pseudo-fine sentence *vox populi vox dei*[1] stand out in its right light!

Common sense is certainly one of the best things in this world—when it is moderately common, if not, it is one of the most stupid things there is!

In reality Goethe wholeheartedly sides with Molière's *Misanthrope*—identifying him with Molière, with himself, and with his best friends. "*Freilich musste er das aus seinem eigenen Busen nehmen, er musste seine eignen Beziehungen gegen die Welt schildern. Und spielst Du nicht dieselbe Rolle gegen Deine Tagsgenossen?*"[2] When was there ever a lover of mankind with a clear head and heart, who was not at the same time and in spite of everything a misanthropist?

p.167,#15 Sense of distance and consciousness of outline! Let them look down upon asceticism with the deepest disdain: it is still the most real starting point for any productive and "spiritual" joy; and no profoundly living person (deep and strong human being) has ever escaped this sting. Here you are confronted with the principle of breaking loose, of concealment, of detour—to which once and for all man's whole joy-hungering mystery is tied—the joy that throws itself in pursuit of timeliness, the world of "openness," "relations," "connections" (exactly where your ultimate connections are severed!) that is the nature of the subservient and trendy ones—but not the human nature.

For a sound, virile, and truly youthful person nothing gives such a feeling of rapture—yes, feeling of eternity—as being able to despise desire.

p.171,#19 The wise breach of faith. It is by all means a question of "dissociating oneself". . . such are the human conditions! But the best

[1]The people's voice, God's voice.
[2]Certainly, he must take that out of his own heart, he must describe his own circumstances vis-à-vis the world. And don't you play the same role in relation to your contemporaries? (Letter to Zelter, 1828).

kind of remoteness and the freest outlook is not attained by means of entertainment, no—on the road of "dullness," on the keen course of Patience!

To tes diaites amikton![1] As if there were any grossness, any treachery   p.172,#22
which, under certain conditions, could be worse than—"polite-ness," "conciliation," "affability!"

And when you have come as far as becoming ecstatic when con-fronted with "the Danish simper"—then, by God, you better pull the covers over your head!

There is no better compass than—fleeing.   p.177,#30
As long as there is something in you that is disgusted with yourself (which flees) you are on a steady course, you are not abandoned.

Captivity—Freedom! *Schola captivitatis!*[2] Was there ever anything   p.178,#33
but the richness of the situation, its *epi xyrou akmes*[3]—in modern terms: "pathology," which came to light in the joy of those whole feelings in accord with the **simple explanation** a diseased and great man of research has given of his life-atmosphere.

"But if I know myself, I work from a sort of instinct to try to make out truth" (Charles Darwin).

Those dedicated to patience. If interpreted in a decisive sense, a   p.179,#34
"friendly Arctic" will be revealed at the innermost depth of nearly everything extreme.

Taste: The great thought of escape. The glacier. Taste is the super-common leveler.

It is the glacier, "the friendly Arctic," the *amikton*, *dysgoēteuton*[4] of taste that alone can make me happy!

These are concrete, firm and happy things: in this great impa-tience and intolerance, in this cultural radicalism, comprehended with dedicated strength, lies my safest world. Here I have felt the power of not doubting a tolerance, an openness, a *honestum*,[5] which

[1]The pure; an unsociable way of life.
[2]The school of captivity.
[3]On a knife's edge.
[4]Pure, hard to enchant.
[5]Honesty.

has stood for my eye in the artful world of thinking as a haven beyond the chimera of convention, and the culture of ostentation. A *honestum* which, however, could never have grown except in the fire of character dilemma and self-rejection. It could never have developed into a culture experience with a rare feeling of certainty—pragmatic, inexhaustible—except under these conditions.

From childhood I was fascinated by Tolstoy and Rousseau—in an era when something affected and twisted artistically, and glamorously fawning, which could never arrive at rightness and justice, never at straight openness of tone—precisely that came to be called tone. I tried to explain, defend myself with that hatred of cowardliness and affectation that my fate and nature had instilled in me. I tried to identify my sins as coming from this source and I would finally be able to say conclusively that my entire development, the history of my character, with its mistakes, absurdities and sins, originated in the loathing of the bootlicker world. I also finally find that only by summoning all my powers of keenness in seeing through the world of bootlickers and cowards have I come to seek defense and explanation.

The New Watchfulness
(posthumous) / 1953

What prevents me from making every day a renewed promise—an p.5,#1 unveiling and disclosure in gratitude of the Life concept? Every day is execution day!

I have weathered some heavy storms. But in its entirety my life has been winged and fleeting.

Don't forget those for whom a sudden terrible experience became p.6,#4 the key to the richness of life and spiritual vision: don't forget them! The boundlessly happy inner expansion that takes place, when the doors to the outer world of desires have to be closed—don't forget!

And in addition to this (if one draws on the future) always to live! Thus being relieved of all anguish of vanity and pride.

The silence of morning's first blush. Where the day will sprout, least p.13,#34 of all can there be any rapacity.

Les premières lueurs.[1] To a great extent the secret of genius lies in the p.17,#47 ability to retrack oneself intuitively to that particular point where one has been unmistakably triumphant. This territory knows no borders—precisely through self-evidence of its reality it is limitless. From there one proceeds, keeping hold of one's happiness, and stands in the light of earliness (*prima luce*).

[1]The first lights.

p.21,#58 He who cherishes the beginning—awaiting himself; is on the track of the art of living.

p.22,#59 You are never any higher—than at a beginning. Better to crawl— than to swell!

p.33,#99 "Where I have a little less than what's strictly necessary, I feel at my best." That is the way it was for Holberg.[1]

    The lightness, the ease! The only quality worthy of worship. How will a human be able to carry his self if not by adoration of the absurdity: the lightness!

p.38,#116 To become accustomed to the incorrigibility of conscience; to be able to foresee the attacks. (Beware of the unexpected, the sudden.)

    Yes, so it has to be.

    And the hope of something useful—of healing words and discovery words—can thus be nourished.

    (Relative honesty . . .)

p.39,#120 The mere thought of the possibility of spiritual freedom should sustain a state of rapture in any sensible human being.

p.40,#121 Everything bears upon the primal light and holy genesis!

    My method of knowledge: nakedness, leanness—to expose myself to the stimulus of light.

    To live for the most absurd of thoughts: this—to be capable of discovering a defense against the darkness!

    The time pattern of the shielding: the Apollonic tempo—the human pace.

p.47,#143 Excitement—search and peace at the same time! A childlike avarice for sights, trails, and traces, and the delight of a sudden faraway view have followed me all through life.

p.70,#213 "When even the whale has his louse," said Goethe once about a persecuting critic, "I'll have to put up with mine"—but rest assured that he would have liked to say the same about many of his praisers!

[1]Celebrated 18th century Danish author.

I was naïve enough to believe that some young and bold person p.88,#266 would one day come up to me reaching out his hand in alliance. I won't live to see that day—but my work will.

Independence has been my predominant passion. How often have I p.97,#292 told myself in weak moments: it has ruined your life! Without it I would have succumbed, before the beginning of my life work; before I had known what joy is.

One should try to get at the root of self-importance, the plague of p.109, #327 self-righteousness, by clearly seeing that they mean death to all productive activity, all refined power influence.

Perhaps eventually, when utterly under pressure, we can free ourselves from the desire to be heard before any authority other than a super-consciousness composed of what is right, redeeming, acquitting. The question could certainly be asked if not every confession is contrived by an actor. A night will come when even the finest feathers I adorn myself with will be painfully plucked.

Rivalries! I could take the stare of the living. But sometimes I have p.121, #361 felt the eyes of the dead looking my way, a stare much harder than the gaze of any contemporary.

The best memory of an enemy-friend sometimes lies in the pang of not having considered the possible ways to knowledge and experience, which could have been taken in the violent, smarting light of a friendship-antagonism.

Ars Magna
(posthumous) / 1954

p.59 The more complete, the simpler your relation to the day, the more deeply eventful and adventurous the power of the meditation.

p.60 The conformity with one's self: this Socratic bliss—*concordia animi*.[1] Nobody has ever achieved it without being considered half-crazy by his contemporaries.

p.61 Nothing holds richer possibilities than to really be in possession of—with one's home in—what one owns.
   Meditation's mine is *esse*.[2]
   What in the Western World is called "concentration" is lameness compared with the Orient's idea of depth, of freedom.

p.62 Observe—breathe—measure. Stick to those. Through them progress is possible.

p.62 In the courage to dedicate oneself to culture, to art, to the highest joy, it is the liberation from self (passivity) that becomes decisive—just as with religion. In this depth of storm the noble bird can build its nest: the bird—Stillness.

p.65 Better the shadow; better departure—to be spared complaining about "the most bitter loneliness under pretense of lots of com-

[1]Unanimity of the soul.
[2]Latin: to be.

pany";[1] not to have to dwell—for nights and days—on the border-line of losing one's mind through disgust for all the cowardly and stupid phrases you listen to yourself, and others express. With all my heart I concur with Kierkegaard's opinion: that children and the aged are the only people who sometimes soothe your mind. From all the so-called intelligent conversations I have witnessed, I would have to try in vain to remember one word worth a single penny. Besides, I have to confess that I generally felt more at ease with the branded and poor unfortunate ones than in so-called "good" company.

[1]Atterbom, 19th century Swedish poet.

The Salt and Helichrysus (posthumous) / 1956

p.26,#35 The greatest beauty in a landscape lies in the peace that can be likened to the stillness of thought's horizon in a deep purposeful eye.

p.36,#63 To find the noblest state of intoxication sometimes struck me as being the aim of any sensible existence, all refinement's secret meaning, and life's inner line of defense. In everything lustreless I divined the symbol and the mystery of the undiscovered, the untrodden ground. Behind all higher education there was for me the holy paradox of a fiery coolness.

p.38,#69 Evenness is the friend of salt—and permanence. Keen and sharp—one day's work after the other!

p.57,#33 On the road to self-knowledge, strongest self-determination, there is no phenomenon in recent history of civilization that has been of greater value to me than Nietzsche. He drove me back to sources of soundness in my nature, and I became his most ardent and grateful antagonist. The music of human enlightenment exposed me to its radiation to the roots of my being.

p.75,#11 Only the defenseless have been the true nurturers of frankness. The paradox was of no use in this world. But in the pragmatism of honest necessity lies a magic that overcomes everything.

The same goes for thought as for art: It is only the necessary that can- p.98,#13
not be refuted. This is precisely referred to as: *"die ergangenen Gedanken."*[1] And therefore only one disease is sickness to death for the
thinker: the one that comes from having evaded necessity's love.

The systems do die, but never the inviolably effective thought.

Thought's seriousness: the possibility of joy. And where lies the p.100,#21
most profound possibility of joy? In the hope of taking oneself seriously. It is about this reality, this pertinence, the struggle has been
fought.

Of all that glitters in this world nothing has exercised a deeper power p.108,#8
on profound minds than—the lusterless.

Because—and don't fool yourself—even in the lackluster there is
a starry sky.

The mildest Necessity—to have been endowed with the healing p.176,#33
power of a sun-enveloped knowledge, to think out, search, learn.

Width and harmony, greatest power of evenness, greatest com- p.185,#17
pounded action: always—*in puncto*![2] Distillation of thought's finest
power: often from the ability to be quietly aware of the preciousness
of the moment.

Magna—perpauca![3]

In the awareness of your conditions lies also your good conscience, your sanction. Assignment of cause always carries strength,
yes, more so: road. A must is a great consolation—a great density.

The precious moment of the day—what is clarity? To have reached
one's clear must.

Particle—and boundlessness; such is the best calm. So it is for a
prisoner, who is certain that he will be able to break out to freedom—
if given only one single day: to be able to look upon one's day in that
light! And still with great calm.

[1]Refers to Nietzsche's words that only those thoughts are of value that have proven
themselves in one's life.
[2]The decisive moment and the compressed expression.
[3]Approximately—macro-micro.

In Silvis Cum Libro
(posthumous) / 1957

p.118,#44 Wherever the early, unpremeditated, and harmless joy of productive life as we know it in our primal and solitary happiness of development can be regained in the expanses and visions of maturity and fuse with their light, there will be found that new, almost somnambular unconcern and security really have their place in all purely productive, ingenious lives.

p.125,#65 The clear wine! Where would weakness have its strength, if not in the pureness of devotion? The only favor he who has come to the end can hope to gain from the scarceness of time is the unclouded happiness of the moment, won by his unconsenting, untrifling, all-exclusive claim to love.

Afterword:
Vilhelm Ekelund—Modernism
and the Aesthetics
of the Aphorism

Vilhelm Ekelund (1880–1949) was an aristocratic and exclusive spirit. He had little respect for members of the academic professions, and he disdained the labels invented by the historians of literature. He would have been shocked had someone called him a Modernist, and literary historians have respectfully refrained from doing so. Nevertheless, despite its title, his *Antikt ideal* (*Ideals of Antiquity*, 1909), in particular the section labeled "*Aforismer till lyrikens själsliv*" ("Aphorisms on the inner life of lyric poetry"), is a radically Modernist document, antedating Pär Lagerkvist's more famous avant-garde manifesto, *Ordkonst och bildkonst* (*The Art of Words and the Art of Painting*), by four years. And although Ekelund neither read nor appreciated Modernist literature, the Modernists obviously read and admired him. For many of them, like the Finnish-Swedish avant-garde poets (Rabbe Enckell, Gunnar Björling), for Pär Lagerkvist, and for the Swedish Modernists of the 1940s and 50s (Tage Aurell, Gunnar Ekelöf, Karl Vennberg, Gösta Oswald, Sven Lindqvist) he became in many ways a mentor and model.[1]

A little-known essay, "Under Damoklessvärdet" ("Under the Sword of Damocles"), written by Olof Enckell and published in the short-lived journal *Quosego* in 1928, gives a good general idea of how the young and very radical Finnish-Swedish poets received Ekelund's works.[2] After an initial declaration of his generation's total lack of interest in contemporary Swedish literature (Hjalmar Bergman, Sigfrid Siwerz, and Anders Österling are among the names listed), Enckell maintains that only two Swedish writers are of major and vital significance, Vilhelm Ekelund and Pär Lagerkvist, intellectual and artistic mentors for the young in an age of revolutionary turmoil. (The historical situation in Finland was vastly different; the country had been torn apart by a civil war.) With respect to Ekelund, it is abundantly clear that it is not the author of *Melodier i skymning* or *Dithyramber i aftonglans*

(*Twilight Melodies* or *Dithyrambs in the Glow of Evening*) that is the focus of Enckell's attention. Edith Södergran was probably influenced by the author of the most exquisitely wrought Symbolist verse in Swedish, but to Enckell and to those for whom he claims to be speaking, it is Ekelund the aphorist, the writer of dense and obscure prose, who really matters.

One word recurs with remarkable frequency in Enckell's generous tribute to Ekelund. It is the word *personlig* ("personal"). What Enckell admires, above all, is Ekelund's uncompromising personal stance, the exclusively personal content of his art, an art that springs from personal necessity and requires a profoundly personal form without any concessions to conventional taste. The gist of Enckell's argument is that Ekelund's art matters because in an age of anxiety and insecurity, of ideological bankruptcy, he has chosen the only visible course: a total commitment to the adventures of the spirit, to the cultivation of a profoundly personal vision, and a profoundly original form, to what Ekelund was later to call *det personliga experimentet* ("the personal experiment").

The virtues extolled by Enckell are obviously those that we associate with the ideology of avant-garde literature and they do, I believe, clearly situate Ekelund within the Modernist tradition, at least in a general way. In this essay I explore Ekelund's achievement and significance more specifically, and in a comparative context, by focusing on what I consider the most important aspect of his Modernism: his commitment to a very special mode of writing, that is, to fragmentary form, more precisely the aphorism. I would argue that Ekelund belongs within an intellectual and literary tradition that includes such disparate but essentially Modernist prose writers as Kierkegaard, Nietzsche, Oscar Wilde, Valéry, Gottfried Benn, Walter Benjamin, and Roland Barthes, a tradition that is characterized by a deliberate movement away from linear and systematic discourse in the direction of fragmentary form of one kind or another (journal, dialogue, collage, aphorism). Another highly significant aspect of this tradition is that most, if not all, of its major representatives have been vitally involved for or against—but mostly for—aestheticism, a fact that has led me to conclude that there exists a close relationship between aestheticism and fragmentary form. While aphorists have not always been aesthetes, a tendency to favor fragmentary form, in particular the aphorism, is, as Susan Sontag has recently maintained, definitely a characteristic of the formalist or aesthetic temperament.[3] Vilhelm Ekelund is no exception to this general rule, and therefore my analysis of his ideas about the nature and function of the aphorism begins with a consideration of his special brand of aestheticism.

The history of aestheticism is still to be written, and there exists no useful general study of the subject. In order to discuss it one must either accept a ready-made definition from a respectable dictionary or develop a workable definition of one's own by examining the ideas generally associated with the tradition. One fact is abundantly clear, however: on the whole aestheticism has had a rather negative critical reception. Effete, sterile, escapist, precious, self-conscious, artificial, and narcissistic above all—these are some of the most common ephithets attached to the word aestheticism. Combine them and they spell decadence, and, in fact, aestheticism is often equated with decadence and hence with such writers as Joris-Karl Huysmans, Oscar Wilde, Aubrey Beardsley, and Gabriele d'Annunzio.

Given such negative connotations, the mere act of associating Vilhelm Ekelund with aestheticism might seem odd, if not absurd, to some, particularly to those who view him as a stern moralist within a radically different tradition of Protestant seriousness. The latter are obviously a strong majority. Lars Gyllensten, for instance, unhesitatingly groups Ekelund with a formidable set of "existential" moralists, among them Luther, Pascal, Ibsen, and Kierkegaard.[4] And K. A. Svensson, Ekelund's "Boswell," subtitles his critical tribute to Ekelund *MoralistenKulturkritikern* (*The Moralist and Culture Critic*) and compares him to other moralist critics such as Pascal, La Rochefoucauld, and Emerson.[5]

In addition, Vilhelm Ekelund's admirers have at times specifically sought to dissociate him from aestheticism. Karl Vennberg's tribute of 1945 may serve as an illustration. Given the title of the essay, "I lydnad under skönheten" ("In Obedience to Beauty"), Vennberg's central argument comes as a distinct surprise.[6] Vennberg argues that in order to understand what is involved in Ekelund's virtually religious devotion to beauty "måste man ha klart för sig att man befinner sig *så långt borta från esteticismen som överhuvud är möjligt*" ("It must be clearly understood that here one is *as far from aestheticism as at all possible*"—[my italics]). "Det sköna," says Vennberg, "är hos Ekelund hunger, fattigdom, samvete" ("The beautiful is for Ekelund hunger, poverty, conscience"). Thus Ekelund's aesthetic concerns are effectively translated into concepts of moral seriousness that were, I presume, easier to accept for a generation as involved with existentialism as the Swedish writers of the 1940s.

Nevertheless, at least one distinguished Swedish critic and literary historian, the late Fredrik Böök, did not hesitate to analyze and evaluate Ekelund's achievement with reference to aestheticism. Böök has been a frequent target of attacks from both the left and the right, but his reputation as a great critic and scholar is secure. The problematic aspect of Böök's criticism is that while his analysis is almost always deft and illuminating, his judgment seems, at least in retrospect, often faulty. His essay on Ekelund is a case in point. It is found in *Resa kring svenska parnassen* (*Journey through the Swedish Helicon*), published in 1926, when Swedish literature was about to change its course in a fundamental manner in conformity with international Modernist trends. The essay reflects Böök's allegiance to bourgeois values, the predominant values of his time and of his class. Böök had no interest in Modernist literature: his aesthetic preferences were embodied in the tradition of Bourgeois Realism.

Böök is unequivocal in his efforts to put the stamp of aestheticism on Ekelund's vision of life and art, which he regards as a form of religion. In contrast to Vennberg's thesis, Böök labels Ekelund's aestheticism "den mest fanatiska, och den mest följdriktiga i vår samtid" ("the most fanatical and the most consistent in our time"), although he admits that "det är ingen bekväm och slapp religion, inriktad på facila njutningar och ytlig tillfredsställelse" ("it is no comfortable and lax religion aimed at facile pleasures and superficial satisfaction"). Ekelund's aestheticism has nothing to do with epicureanism, says Böök; it is a demanding "gospel" requiring self-denial, discipline, and moderation, ultimately even a total surrender of self. Ekelund's cult of beauty is, in fact, analogous to the cult of the basic Christian virtues.[7]

Having granted Ekelund "allvar och storhet" ("solemnity and greatness"), Böök proceeds to stress the serious limitations of what he calls Ekelund's "förkunnelse" or gospel. It is, he argues, a limited, narcissistic, and sterile gospel, an anomaly. Böök sees Ekelund as a pietist and a quietist, not unlike Thomas à Kempis or Kierkegaard, to whom the cult of inwardness is all, and he deplores Ekelund's scorn for external life and his utter indifference to social life, to social norms, and to human companionship. Like his mentor Nietzsche, Ekelund is seen as committed to an "aesthetic idealism" that is tainted by fanaticism, arrogance, and inhumanity.

As so often, Böök is both right and wrong. Ekelund's aestheticism is indeed of a radical variety and there is a religious fervor attached to his total commitment to art. His only real commitment is to writing and to the building of the self—not to any social or moral ends. Cultivating the aesthete's ideal of detachment, Ekelund's mode of writing is hermetic, directed to the select few. Nevertheless, Böök's negative critique is invalid because it is based on false assumptions. To attribute a "gospel" to Ekelund is wrong, for he had a most definite animus against dogmas (including the central Christian dogmas) and systems of thought: he is a psychologist, not a philosopher. Furthermore, unlike Kierkegaard, whose Christianity is above all a single-minded devotion to inwardness, Ekelund seeks an integration of inwardness and sensuousness, of art and life. Finally, Böök fails to recognize that the exclusiveness of a writer's style or mode need not preclude significant impact on other human beings if they are sufficiently receptive.[8]

In defense of Böök, one ought to remember that he based his judgment on Ekelund's writings prior to 1926. There are those who would argue that Ekelund's "world" was essentially formed by that time, but I believe they are mistaken: he continued to develop and refine his ideas and concepts, and he died at the peak of his powers. The aspects of his aestheticism that I think of as the most positive are, in my view, much more apparent in the later texts (that is, from the mid-1930s on). I doubt whether Böök would have detected the change, for his strictures on aestheticism are not uncommon and reflect, I believe, a fundamental failure of perception.

The roots of the problem lie, possibly, in the fact that there are two different modern forms of aestheticism. One I label the *formalist* or purist mode. It involves, above all, a great stress on the autonomous structure and form of art. The second, I prefer to call the *ludic* mode. Its fundamental ideas may be traced to Schiller's *Letters on the Aesthetic Education of Man*. It stresses aesthetic activity as a form of gratuitous and festive play, as an end in itself. Its ideal is wholeness, the integration of sensuousness and spirit, and its goal is freedom. In addition, it places much emphasis on joy and pleasure. Within the Modernist tradition its major representatives include Nietzsche, Wilde, Gide, Thomas Mann, Valéry, Ortega y Gasset, and Roland Barthes.

Ekelund's aestheticism encompasses both varieties. He is most definitely a strict formalist and purist. This aspect of his work has also been the subject of ample commentary. The ludic element, particularly in his later texts, has largely been ignored. In the following analysis of some of Ekelund's major themes and concepts I shall place a greater emphasis on the ludic mode, particularly in view of its importance with respect to Ekelund's choice of the aphorism as his exclusive mode of writing. The aphorism is, it may be argued, the ludic form of expression *par excellence*.

In a recent interview, published in the student newspaper *The Daily Californian*, the French philosopher Michel Foucault argues that "what we are looking for is . . . an ethics which could in itself be an aesthetics of existence."[9] Referring to the ancient Greeks as having such an ethics, "an ethics which has nothing to do with religion or science, but with aesthetics," he also cautions that he is of course not suggesting "that we have to begin again to live like the Greeks." The precise implications of Foucault's remarks are not clear to me but the general idea has a striking resemblance to what I perceive to be Ekelund's major objective. The main body of Ekelund's prose work consists of criticism, and this criticism takes the form of a continuous quest, the subject of which is aesthetics, to him, sadly enough, the most neglected and perhaps even the most despised of all sciences. And Ekelund too, true to the teachings of Nietzsche, concluded early on that it was the Greeks "som gifvit de bästa uttrycken, de bästa, mest upplysande formuleringarna och bestämmelserna af hvad som för människosinnet är eftersträfvansvärdt" ("who have given the best expressions, the best, most illuminating wordings and definitions of that worth striving for by the human spirit") (A:158–59).[10]

In a significant aphorism in *Metron*, Ekelund questions himself about the value of aesthetic studies. One answer he might have given is that aesthetics is the study of beauty, important enough, because "det vackra är ju det enda, som det är någon glädje med i lifvet" ("beauty is certainly the only thing that gives joy to life") (M:89). More significantly, however, the study of aesthetics provides us with valuable knowledge, knowledge about man's deepest needs and desires and about the ways to wholeness. Aesthetics is for Ekelund the science that most effectively discloses the ways to positive and liberating states of mind, to joy and productivity. As such it obviously has nothing to do with a withdrawal from life; on the contrary, it offers the means to its enhancement.

This remarkable emphasis on the study of aesthetics as the avenue to a clearer conception of what it means to lead a full life is also reflected in Ekelund's high estimation of art and its power, an estimation he shares with Nietzsche. Nietzsche, at least in his earlier writings, celebrated art as a metaphysical palliative, as nothing less than a justification of existence, arguing that art alone confers value on a nature that is in itself without value. Ekelund, true to his Skåne heritage, shuns all metaphysical speculations, insisting instead on the paradigmatic nature of art, that is, on art as a model for an ideal, truly satisfying mode of existence. Art, he argues, has nothing to do with *prakt* ("splendor") or *makt* ("power"); it is a pragmatic (*pragmatisk*) guide to the art of living. The so-called "gift of the Muses" means, he says, essentially this: that if someone wishes to lead a full life he must learn to live on art, that is, to turn life into art. The real task in life is to relate to the world in the manner of an artist. Ekelund quotes with approval what he calls Goethe's "masterly interpretation" of man's true destiny: "die eigentliche Aufgabe des Lebens: dass der Mensch sich zu *allen* ausser ihm liegenden Dingen wie ein Künstler verhalte, der aus dem vorgefundenen Stoffe ein Werk seines Geistes macht" ("what life is really about: that man acts in relation to all things as would an artist who through his spirit creates a work from existing materials") (E:47–48). To live like an artist is, in fact, not an ideal confined to artists; it is a paradigm for all human beings: "Att såsom diktande lefva (hvilket i grunden gäller för oss alla) är att förtäta lifvet" ("To live as a poet—which is basically valid for all of us—is to densify [intensify] life") (E:100).

The aphorism just cited raises some fundamental questions as to the specific meanings Ekelund attaches to words such as "art" and "artist." *Täthet*, generally meaning "density," "compactness," is one of Ekelund's most cherished concepts and, like many other concepts of his, it remains opaque because of the complexity of meanings attached to it. Basically, *täthet* signifies density and brevity in a strictly rhetorical sense. Like Goethe, Ekelund has a fondness for etymological games and in an effort to define his own preference for lapidary modes of writing he quotes Goethe's playful association *"dicht—dichten* (spissare, densare)" (E:99). He then goes on to apply the same concept to the art of living: "Dagen själf—bästa dikt! Men *tät* skall den vara. Tät—som hvarje god dikt!" ("The day itself—the best poem! But it has to be dense. Dense—like any good poem!") (E:100). Here the meaning has shifted to an existential level: *täthet* is a paradigm for an ideal form of existence, implying fullness, wholeness, order, intensity.

Art, then, obviously has to do with *form*, on a rhetorical as well as on an existential level. But art is also associated with the concept of *lek*, of play, a concept fundamental to an understanding of Ekelund's concern with productivity and with *joy* as the touchstone for the quality of human activities. The central significance of the concept of play with respect to the problem of productivity is clearly evident in the following aphorisms:

• *The master stroke of economy is always to turn the serious into play and play into the serious. "Happiness follows lust—pleasure," it is said. As a writer one cannot have better conditions! Provided one really has the strength to fulfill those conditions, make one's self fit for them. (AH:67)*

• *The most precious truths are those that befall man at play, as* musicus. *Play is the basic stimulus. Play: the great economy. "Man muss dem Schicksal nicht merken lassen, was man will." [One should not give fate the opportunity to know what one wants]—Nietzsche. Yes, at that time he was on the road of quietism! Of quietism: of the human economy. (PS:111)*

• Patiens—vigil *[patient—watchful]: to will . . . and* not *to will. What does Orpheus signify? That will to power is will to music. Only the one with the cool hands shall lift the treasure. All things draw close to whoever shelters the right music. (PS:110–11)*

• *Play, the artistic play without intended gain—home of the real freedom of movement! All productive people have in their best attitude been distinguished by such aimlessness, childishness, somnambulism—not least the great workers! Only in this way dubiousness with regard to* consistency *has found its true solution. Nothing demands firmer boundaries than such softness, such absence of method!—no stricter containment than such freedom. And work-pride is a concept, concept of pathos, which artistic man has to watch—and watch out for. (AH:63)*

A reader familiar with Ekelund's vocabulary will immediately recognize the allusions to some of his key concepts: *ekonomi, musik, grund, quietism, rörelse, frihet, afsiktslöshet* (economy, music, foundation [ground], quietism, movement, freedom, aimlessness [purposelessness]). The major concern is how to remain productive in the matters of the spirit. Hence the vital importance of economics, of means and methods, of "nourishment." Here the argument centers around a paradox: the best results are achieved by the very absence of method, that is, by *play*. The secret lies in *afsiktslöshet* (aimlessness), that is, the absence of design, of set purpose, which, in turn, is analogous to *musik* (music), one of Ekelund's most important terms. *Lek, afsiktslöshet*, and *musik* (play, aimlessness, and music) are obviously analogous concepts. Their counterpart is will. Nothing of value, certainly not wisdom or truth, is to be gained by will, by design, by system.

It is interesting to note that these aphorisms appear in the context of an ongoing polemic against Nietzsche:

- *Would one be ready for the discovery that Nietzche's creative element is to be found in his pure aphoristics? That his "science" ranks only second—and not even that! Because between the two lies his—by no means ordinary—poetry. (PS:121)*

- *The tension, the oneness, life interplay: precisely by virtue of the anciently pragmatic, the prehistorically unmethodic! When Nietzsche steps beyond himself and his protective defense, and becomes a "theoretician," an intention thinker, a calculation thinker—he is rendered skinless. (PS:120)*

There are numerous aspects to Ekelund's critique of Nietzsche, a rich subject requiring extensive analysis, but the most central is undoubtedly his contention that Nietzsche's decline began when he developed his ideas about "the will to power." Here Ekelund clearly implies that once upon a time Nietzsche too knew the secret of *real* power. "*Den gången*" refers, I believe, to the period when Nietzsche wrote his most joyful and exuberant works—works like *Fröhliche Wissenschaft (The Gay Science)* with its exquisite aphorisms and dancing songs celebrating the bracing mistral and the life of "Prince Vogelfrei." This, the "gentle" Nietzsche, is obviously Ekelund's ideal, the Nietzsche who admired Epicurus, Horace, Montaigne, and Goethe, and celebrated art and the artist and the *vita contemplativa*. During this period Nietzsche had neither a system of thought nor a method and engaged in a most unconventional mode of philosophizing. In his final phase, however, when dogma and theory supplanted art, Nietzsche wrote in a more conventional mode offering arguments in defense of his doctrines (the theory of the Eternal Recurrence, for instance). In the process he also became—like any other theorist—"vulnerable."

Closely related themes, again obviously inspired by reading Nietzsche, are developed in the next two aphorisms:

- *The joy of thinking: the joy of wandering. For the contemplative there has never been any other way. It is the genuine, the **pragmatic** way of a wanderer's thought that Lessing expressed in his famous words: "Nicht durch den Besitz, sondern durch die Nachforschung der Wahrheit erweiten sich des Menschen Kräfte." [Not through its possession but by the search for truth human powers are unfolding.]*

    A wanderer's thought contra—paid thought! Thoughts while wandering contra—with the intent of gain! (AH:61)

• *To search—not by virtue of love for something desired, a result, a gain; to search—by virtue of love for the search itself: that is music. /PAIZEIN EN KALOIS/ In relation to the divine, man is the child who tries to imitate by playing the earnest activities of grownups. And that is what divinity demands of us: to be playing beautifully. (BL:99)*

Ekelund, like Nietzsche, is a peripatetic thinker—even in a literal sense. Nietzsche once maintained that you can tell how thoughts were born, whether in a cramped position by a desk or during a brisk walk in the open air.[12] Some of his most liberated ideas were also hatched during his walks in the Swiss mountains or by the Mediterranean Sea in Genoa. Ekelund, we know, was an avid walker. But both Ekelund and Nietzsche are also peripatetic thinkers in a metaphorical sense. They are both "free spirits" in Nietzsche's sense of the term. A number of central themes in Ekelund's works converge in this context. On the most concrete level, "vandrartanke" (a wanderer's thought) is contrasted to "lönetanke" (paid thought), involving the rejection of fame and gain as motivating forces in life and thought. Ekelund always conceived of the ideal mode as the privilege "att icke behöfva skrifva annat än för sin egen tillfredsställelse och tillväxande" (not having to write except for one's own satisfaction and growth) (AH:92).

On another level, the ideal of the thinker as wanderer is a synthesis of ideas derived from Nietzsche's writings during the 1880s, including *The Wanderer and His Shadow* and *The Dawn of Day*, ideas ultimately embodied in the image of the "free spirit." The "free spirit" is for Nietzsche, as W. D. Williams has defined it, "the epitome . . . of the intelligence operating entirely on its own terms, unhindered by tradition or morality, or even logic, the ideal of pure mental activity unswayed by passion or loyalty or any other extra-intellectual motive."[13] As the allusion to Lessing reveals, a specific conception of truth is at the heart of this dialectical or process-oriented thought. Like Nietzsche, and like Kierkegaard before him, Ekelund echoes Lessing's famous dictum that if God held the possession of truth in his right hand and in his left the lifelong pursuit of it, he (Lessing) would choose the left.[14] This dictum, which as we know became the cornerstone of Kierkegaard's thesis that truth is subjectivity and thus the foundation for modern Existentialism, also embodies Ekelund's conception of truth. Like the Existentialists, Ekelund seeks to reconcile life and knowledge, thought and action, placing an exclusive emphasis on *lived* thought, *experienced* thought, *earned* thought. The goal is not an end; it is to remain on the road, to make life into a quest, a perpetually renewed adventure of the spirit. For Ekelund, as for Nietzsche, the real value of an individual depends on his ability "to give to quotidian experience the stamp of the eternal."[15] "*Dagen för dagens skull*" (The day for the sake of the day) is also one of Ekelund's central themes (AH:89). "Hvardag" (the everyday) is "äfventyr" (adventure) and "det närmaste" (the closest) is "flykt" (flight) (AH:75).

That the unconventional mode of the "free spirit," the thinker without method or design, is fraught with risks and dangers is apparent to Ekelund. Consequently, while he repeatedly stresses that a strong "Bohemian" trait is the characteristic of *all* truly creative and inventive individuals, he also insists that those without method develop a "preparedness" (*bereddhet*) and exercise a profound discipline. These provide the necessary continuity and form: "Intet skänker ett sådant sammanhang åt lifvet som att lefva i en bereddhet för det oväntades lycka. Det är lockbetet—äfventyrskänslan—som är det viktigaste för den omethodiske" (Nothing gives such coherence to life as to live in preparedness for the joy of the unexpected. It is the bait—the feeling of adventure—which is most essential for the one without method) (AH:80). Using a combination of allusions to Shakespeare, Nietzsche ("Nur die ergangenen Gedanken haben Wert"—"Only thoughts reached by walking have value"), and Voltaire ("chez soi"—"at home"), Ekelund summarizes his thoughts in two compact aphorisms:

- Readiness is all. *One owns the thought one has wandered: one owns the thought for which one has prepared oneself. One owns the thought for which one is—at home! (AH:66)*
- *Man is a fragment. Therefore his predestination is preparedness.* Readiness is all. *(AH:67)*

"Bereddhet for det oväntades lycka" ("Preparedness for the joy of the unexpected"), receptivity, readiness, for the rapture of the unexpected: it is difficult not to notice Ekelund's fondness for the word *lyckan*. It is a difficult word to translate: at times it suggests luck, at other times joy, sometimes (as here) it spells a form of bliss or rapture of an almost mystical nature. Ekelund frequently resorts to the discourse of mysticism in his efforts to describe the way to truth and wisdom. Gradually, such key concepts as play, music, and art become practically synonymous with the word *mystik*, mysticism. To return to an earlier aphorism (*"Patiens—vigil"*), it is interesting to note the allusions to *quietism* and to Orpheus. In this context the language of mysticism is tied to the beautiful image of *de svala händerna*, the cool hands, and to *skatten*, the treasure, the implication being that "the treasure" (whatever great value that might be) is not to be gained through an exercise of the will but through a form of gratuitous play tempered by a special receptivity shaped by inner discipline. For Ekelund truth is not to be gained by an unveiling or by delving deeply: it is an unexpected gift, a lucky find, a treasure captured by surprise or not at all. It is bestowed on those who are prepared and deserving and they, in turn, are the only ones who can bestow it on others.

There are, as Ekelund emphasizes, echoes of both Eastern and Western mysticism in these ideas. Again, Ekelund is by no means unique in his tendency to employ the language of mysticism in his discourse. The tendency of aestheticism and mysticism to converge in some of the major Modernist writers has not escaped the attention of at least one major critic.[16] We need only recall Proust and his timeless essences, Joyce and his epiphanies, and the curious blend of mystic and aesthetic components in T. S. Eliot's *Four Quartets*. Taoist ideas have influenced Swedish Modernist writers like Gunnar Ekelöf and Harry Martinson during some phases of their careers. The most striking illustration is perhaps to be found in the autobiography of Roland Barthes, *Barthes on Barthes*. In one of his many efforts to define "bliss," Barthes writes: "Bliss is not what *corresponds to* desire (what satisfies it) but what surprises, exceeds, disturbs, deflects it." To find the perfect formulation of this thought he has to turn to mystics, to Jan van Ruysbroek, who wrote: "I call intoxication of the mind that state in which pleasure exceeds the possibilities which desire had entertained."[17] Ekelund could well have written that.

On the whole, no other factor illustrates more effectively Ekelund's radical break with the German-Scandinavian tradition of high moral seriousness than his repeated celebrations of the great delight of the free exercise of consciousness unhampered by moral, political, or religious passions. In the Scandinavian context, in which major writers such as Kierkegaard, Ibsen, and Strindberg have been profoundly ambivalent in their attitudes toward art, Ekelund is unique in his unequivocal affirmation of the principles of art for art's sake and of the ludic desire in all intellectual activity of value. The consequence of such a radical form of aestheticism, of such an exclusive cultivation of blissful states of consciousness, is, as might be expected, a total indifference to history. One searches in vain for the merest reflection of the terrors and horrors of the century, recalling that the period from World War I to 1949 was indeed a turbulent and traumatic age. For this indifference to the sufferings of a tragic age he has also been chastised by his severest critics. With respect to the study of literature, Ekelund's attitude is also profoundly nonhistorical. Like Nietzsche he regards the historical sense (Nietzsche's "sixth sense") as critical and pragmatic, its function being to assess the value of the past in terms of its ability to serve the vital needs of the living. However, unlike Nietzsche, whose paradigmatic heroes are often men of action (Napoleon, Julius Caesar), Ekelund looks to the great writers and thinkers of the past for practical guidance and support in matters of art and of the intellect.[18]

Consistency, *följdriktighet*, is a virtue often praised by Ekelund. His aim is to harmonize thought and action and art and life. That he should seek a mode of expression uniquely adapted to the nature of his project consequently comes as no surprise. And if we boldly and quickly summarize the basic ideas of Ekelund's aestheticism—the emphasis on artistry and on the ludic spirit; the resistance to theory and design; the idea of the peripatetic thinker, the free spirit, always ready to move on in quest of new beginnings; the love of the quotidian, of the day; the insistence on joy and bliss and on thought as a kind of gift—neither does it come as a surprise that the aphorism should be his choice of form. A highly compact and concentrated mode of expression, it is certainly an intensely artistic form; but it is also singularly open-ended and fluid, like lyric poetry resisting paraphrase and systematization. Its provisional and fragmentary quality makes it the ideal vehicle for peripatetic thought, and for someone who believes that truths may only be glimpsed or caught by surprise. As a form it obviously bears a close relationship to the journal, the mode that records the events of the day and the texture of the quotidian. It is, finally, a ludic form whose aesthetic delight is engendered by the verbal texture itself, by wit, allusion, and paradox.

Nevertheless, although Ekelund at a relatively early stage had come to the conclusion that criticism must be a form of art, a variety of considerations, not the least of them economic, kept him from turning to the aphorism on an exclusive basis.[19] Until the year 1925, when the remarkable volume *Lefnadsstämning* (*Mood of Life*) was published, Ekelund's works were a blend of aphorisms and more conventional literary essays. The steps in the process that gradually led him to abandon, first, lyric poetry, and, second, the essay in favor of the aphorism are significant and shed light on the development of his general aesthetic principles.[20]

På hafsstranden (1922) contains Ekelund's last lyric poems. Henceforth he would turn his attention to prose, alternating for some time between the essay, the prose poem, and the aphorism. That it was Nietzsche who steered him in this direction is beyond doubt. By 1907, Nietzsche had become his Bible, a source of "lärdom, styrka, tröst" ("learning, strength, solace"), and most definitely his mentor in aesthetic matters.[21] Nietzsche's own works proved conclusively that it was possible to be "en stor tankediktare på prosa" ("a great poet of ideas writing in prose").[22] He also gave Ekelund the courage to accept the consequences of such an ambition for a modern writer. Lack of recognition and loneliness are the inevitable consequences of a writer's refusal to satisfy the desires of a bourgeois reading public accustomed to realistic novels and a musical poetry of sentiment. Ekelund quotes with approval a few significant lines by Nietzsche: "Bist du ein Stern? So musst du auch wandern wollen, du Unstäter, und ohne Heimat sein" ("Are you a star? Then you must also wish to wander, a vagrant, and be without a homeland").[23]

Most importantly, it was obviously Nietzsche who guided Ekelund in the direction of the most exclusive of prose forms, the aphorism, a form in which he had attained great mastery. Ekelund had read other aphorists, we know, notably the German George Chr. Lichtenberg, and some of the great French masters like Chamfort and La Rochefoucauld, but his own style bears greater resemblance to Nietzsche's, and his general ideas about the role and function of the aphorism are definitely derived from Nietzsche. The polemical tone, the fondness for paradox, the philological discourse, the blend of conceptual and metaphorical language: these are some of the pronounced similarities of style. Ekelund must certainly have been encouraged by Nietzsche's unabashed assertions about the superiority of the aphorism, a form in which you can express in ten sentences what others do not even manage in a book. It is a demanding form, demanding for the writer and equally demanding for the reader, but it is capable of producing the most profound and inexhaustible books (like Pascal's . *ensées*). Above all, it is a form of great artistic perfection.

By the early 1920s, Ekelund was ready for a new phase in his career, this time involving a total commitment to aphoristic form. "Det gick mig med böcker ungefär som det vid slutet af min första diktarfas gick mig med landskapet och naturen. Jag slutade att *skildra* och *redogöra*: och då först blef mig det ena som det andra till näring, till lif" ("It happened to me with books more or less as it happened to me with landscape and nature at the end of my first stage as a poet. I stopped describing and reporting: only then one thing after another came alive, became nourishment") (A:59). In a caustic aphorism from 1919, the typical essay comes in for some harsh criticism: "Essayn är i allmänhet intet annat än konsten att prätta upp gamla kläder och inbilla folk att de är nya" ("Generally the essay is nothing but the art of ripping apart old clothes and making people believe they are new") (A:117). The essay and the aphorism ought to be the sovereign modes, "den lifligaste och rörligaste af alla litterära former" ("the most lively and flexible of all literary forms"), but it is obvious that the essay form has degenerated, leaving the aphorism as the only viable form for a select audience. "Karaktärsmålningar" ("character development") may be left to the novelist: the superior art is the art of the aphorist who can provide *karaktärsutsikter* ("character portraits") with a few quick strokes. "Aforistikern," says Ekelund finally, "är de läskunnigas diktare (Ty diktningen i allmänhet är dock mer och mindre beräknad på de icke-läskunniga)" (The writer of aphorisms is the writer for the literate [For anyway, writing is generally more or less intended for the illiterate]).

The distinction between an art for a "literate" as opposed to an "illiterate" public is now of central significance for Ekelund and it recurs in a remarkable aphorism from 1925 that serves to establish the general principles of a functional aesthetic of the aphorism. Although worded in a general and somewhat tentative language, the aphorism signals Ekelund's future commitment to a cryptic mode of discourse, a difficult mode of writing, fostering a new appreciation for language and a new and closer relationship to a special kind of reader:

> *The industrialization of the spirit, as it becomes more and more predominant, will create disgust and contempt for the written word. From this in time will grow a cryptic mode of writing. Because love of the genuine will increase proportionately, be refined and spiritualized. The urge for a deep relationship with the reader will grow. Lucky is the author who is capable of preparing himself for such obscurity and is wise enough to be content with it.*
> *(L:136–37)*

Intrinsically the aphorism is not a cryptic form of discourse. Most aphorisms (of the general type included in W. H. Auden's and Louis Kronenberger's anthology, for instance) are very accessible and may be readily assimilated by an intelligent reader.[24] Of Ekelund's aphorisms written after 1925, some do belong to this general type, but as a rule they are growing increasingly obscure. One consequence of this development was that, from the 1930s on, Ekelund could no longer count on having his books published by a leading publisher but had to rely on special funding for a printing of small editions (often no more than 500 copies). By 1949, at the time of his death, it seemed natural that the first doctoral dissertation devoted to the study of Ekelund's works was a stylistic and cryptological analysis presenting the first systematic effort at interpreting his private and difficult language.[25]

We know Ekelund's justification for a cryptic mode of discourse. It remains for us to examine the elements that contribute to the opacity so characteristic of his later works.

In his many aphorisms reflecting on the very nature and function of the aphorism, Ekelund, not surprisingly, insists on the superiority of a form of art that stresses the virtues of brevity and density. To Ekelund superior art is analogous to a lapidary and laconic mode, and the only authentic writers are those who "icke gripit till pennan utom då de åsyftat ett lifsuttryck af full pregnans" ("have not resorted to the pen unless their aim was a life expression of full pregnancy") (E:102). The acid test of a writer's worth, the proof of how well he has filled his days, is not a long row of books, but thoughts brought to fruition. Emerson, a writer whose works at one point greatly inspired Ekelund, is ultimately regarded as a failure because of his predilection for "helgjutna" ("consummate"), that is, highly composed essays. "Provisoriskt, empraktiskt: så det bästas—och *varaktigas* karaktär" ("Provisional, pragmatic: that is the character of the best—of the most durable"), Ekelund insists in a characteristically paradoxical formulation (AH:104).

While brevity and density obviously contribute to a certain degree of opacity, they are also integral aspects of aphoristic form in general. In order to assess Ekelund's unique achievement with respect to the aphoristic mode we have to examine his practice, not his statements. A detailed analysis is out of the question: a few general observations will have to suffice.

The uniqueness of Ekelund's aphoristic style resides, I would argue, in his progressive tendency to make language both the substance and the texture of his reflections on art and life. The remarkable degree of opacity inherent in his texts springs in turn from his growing predilection for indulging himself in elaborate and highly sophisticated philological games. This fondness, finally, is but a realization in practice of a conclusion he had evidently arrived at as early as the year 1919, when in an aphorism—significantly enough, including a tribute to his philological mentor Nietzsche—he stated unequivocally that "språk är filosofi" ("language is philosophy") (A:158– 59).

Philology implies a method of sorts but in Ekelund's case the term "method" is inappropriate for he is definitely a playful rather than a systematic thinker. At times his discourse might appear like a form of semantic analysis but it soon becomes obvious that he is not really interested in the precise definition of meaning and that his approach is poetic rather than analytical.

Four closely interrelated aspects of Ekelund's philological excursions serve to compound the difficulties involved in any effort to decipher his more complex texts: 1) his focus on a set of private concepts; 2) his elaborate etymologies; 3) his fondness for paradoxical formulations; and 4) his allusiveness, that is, his frequent and often oblique references to other literary texts.

1) A reader familiar with Ekelund's works can recite a long list of the concepts that occur with the greatest frequency: *låghet, täthet, gräns, charis, öga, metron, början, färd, morgon, gruva, musik, nyhet, salt, tydlighet* (lowliness, density, boundary, charis, eye, metron, beginning, journey, morning, mine, music, newness, salt, lucidity), and so on. These concepts, which are all central to his research in aesthetics, are handled in an unsystematic manner and any effort to define them with precision is bound to fail. What confronts the reader is a series of seemingly open-ended improvisations with Ekelund circling playfully around his favorite concepts, elaborating temporarily on their potentialities of meaning before moving on to a new topic. *Början* (beginning) and *nyhet* (newness) are, interestingly enough, two of Ekelund's key concepts, indicating his love of beginnings, of fresh starts and approaches. His work with concepts might be characterized just so: as a series of ever-renewed raids on words in search of new or deeper or more complex meanings. The result is also a steady growth of complex signification. Thus the word *täthet* (density), for instance, which we have already encountered as a special term of praise with respect to form ("en tät dikt"—"a dense poem") and to the art of living ("en tät dag"—"a dense day"), gradually expands its meaning until it finally comes to signify intensity, that is, the highest degree, of meaning. Which is probably another way of saying that it signifies—opacity.

2) For the reader without an extensive knowledge of foreign languages, Ekelund's aphorisms pose difficulties, for many of his philological excursions take the form of elaborate etymologies bringing into play a very large vocabulary including words and texts from a variety of foreign languages, especially German, English, and Italian, as well as Greek and Latin. Again it should be stressed that these linguistic exercises are essentially ludic in nature. Ekelund is not really intent on tracing the development of his favored concepts in order to disclose their true or original meaning.

3) An additional sign of Ekelund's linguistic playfulness is his steadily growing fondness for paradox, for the oxymoron in particular, a predilection he undoubtedly inherited from Nietzsche. I am thinking here of such playful Nietzschean formulations as "Diese Griechen waren oberflächlich— aus Tiefe" (Those Greeks were superficial in a—deep sense), which might be compared to a typical aphorism by Ekelund:

> *Exactly by means of these characteristics: density, compression, weight [all that the Greeks called density/coarseness] you may avoid appearing strained! Whether you will succeed in saying a word of wisdom, of grace, of—lightness, depends precisely upon possessing that quality. (PS:5)*[26]

4) Ekelund is essentially a literary critic, not a creative writer (which does not mean that he is not an artist!). He is very fond of the word *erfarenhet*, experience, but the experience to which he is referring is wisdom derived from the reading of great writers: Plato, Homer, Shakespeare, Montaigne, Goethe, Nietzsche, etc. This is reflected in his habitual tendency to use allusions, to fabricate texts based on other texts, a phenomenon that today would be labeled intertextuality. Again it should be stressed that this predilection for intertextuality is primarily ludic in nature, a fact underscored by Ekelund himself in the following (in itself etymologically playful) defense of the art of allusion: "I allt fint spel är det anspelningen, som är det finaste" (In all fine play it is the allusion that is the finest) (E:78–79). Or in a slightly different formulation: "Allusion kan vara ett vissnadt intellekts sista konstgrepp och sista hjälpmedel. Allusion kan vara fackla, och hög: som konsten" (Allusion may be a withered intellect's last artifice and aid. Allusion may be a torch—and tall as art) (E:97–98).

The following aphorism, part of a series under the general heading *"Accidit in puncto quid non speratur in anno"* (a quotation from Martial), is of interest for two reasons. First, it illustrates the highly self-contained and self-reflective nature of much of Ekelund's writings, celebrating the very strengths of his own special form of lapidary discourse. Second, it allows us to observe the effective interplay of all the elements discussed above, that is, the intense signification of private concepts, the etymologies (toying with the origins of the word aphorism in a Greek verb roughly meaning to limit, mark off, define), the oxymorons, and the allusions (Horace, Shakespeare):

The profession and art of the sayers—insofar as passion is involved, namely the art of those who did not seize the pen unless their aim were a life expression of the fullest pregnancy—must by all necessity lead to a search for the laws of human economy. Their acquisition of character (the art of chan- neling life) is the process of the fruit ripening, growing transparent from self- knowing: self research beyond the conditions of limit and distance necessary for liberation of the most blissful energies. They are all perpauca lo- quentes [speaking in few words]: lapidaric—and expansive.

The great voyages of exploration have been undertaken in nuce (at the core)—"In a nut-shell"—says Shakespeare-Hamlet. And the true, joyous light of an aphorismēnon—is also exactly what the word says: the one of separateness. If, of all literary forms, the aphorism is the one most pro- foundly limited, this would also indicate that—in order to have any meaning —it is also the most profoundly limiting form and as such precisely—unlim- ited. (Di bene fecerunt, inopis me quodque pusilli finxerunt animi, raro et perpauca loquentis.) [Hor., Serm., I.4: The gods did well who made me poor and insignificant at heart, rarely speaking and in few words.] (E:102–3)

After this, it is hardly surprising to note how Ekelund, in an even more glowing tribute to the artistic virtues of the aphorism, stresses the *festive*, that is, the joyous and playful, nature of a form that, for him, ideally hovers some- where between speech and silence:

The living light protects, the living light—hides. The whole artistic char- acter of the aphorism, its festivum [festive joy] lies in its openness—tight- ness, its character of said—unsaid—"sounding silence."

Antiquity is future. To the extent that the aphorism has been antiquity's mode of thought, it is also the future's. It expresses the "catholic" ideal— without a native country—by means of its openness, lacking shores: the lim- itless onwards, contained in all pure, human moderation. (AH:97)[27]

To flirt with silence is to push a literary genre to its extreme limits (as radi- cally Modernist writers do). For Ekelund it amounts to a realization of his primary aesthetic objectives: to write for a select, "literate" audience, and, in the process, "to purify the language of the tribe," to quote Mallarmé. Thus a quality that to some would be a sign of arrogant disdain for the ordinary reader is transformed into a distinct virtue. Admittedly, reading a large num- ber of conventional aphorisms can be like paying a visit to an art museum and seeing too many masterpieces one after the other: a sense of surfeit quickly arises. The very difficulty of Ekelund's fragments serves to preclude this response. The reader who chooses to confront the challenges posed by the texts soon discovers that there is no easy way to decipher them. There is no obvious message to be paraphrased, every aphorism reflects an anterior discourse to be discovered and absorbed, and some concepts are only to be grasped by intuition. The reader must in fact join in the game, retrace the steps, make the author's quest his own. It is in this sense that Ekelund can insist that the aphorism is "den pragmatiska litterära formen, *par excellence.* Vandrartanke—contra lönetanke" (the pragmatic literary form par excellence: the wanderer's thought versus paid thought), the peripatetic thinker's ideal mode of expression (PS:115). The benefit and the pleasure we derive from the form are equal to the effort we are willing to make. The apprehension of the form is inseparable from the apprehension of the thought.

Again, we must note Ekelund's remarkable predilection for consistency. Recalling his particular conception of truth, his belief that the quest for truth is an end in itself, we note that this conception is reflected in a form of expression that requires, in effect, that truths be *earned.* "Nur die ergangenen Gedanken haben Wert" (Only thoughts reached by walking have value) is a maxim of Nietzsche's quoted with approval by Ekelund.[28] His own, "Böcker måste lefvas för att läsas" (Books must be lived to be read), conveys a similar thought (BL:23). It is in this sense that the few who choose to become involved in the process discover that reading Ekelund can be a profound adventure of the spirit. In this context it is interesting to note that those scholars who have commented on Ekelund's affinities with Eastern schools of thought, notably Buddhism, have failed to observe some very significant similarities with regard to the relationship between a particular form of cryptic discourse and the apprehension of truth. What the French critic Robert Linssen has to say about the so-called Koan exercises that form the instruction in Zen Buddhism may well be applied to Ekelund's aphorisms: "The lack of precise and rigid ideas, which is criticized by some, forces sincere seekers to find experiences of a far more individual and profound character than those suggested by the too perfect and systematized codifications of a text."[29] Here again we may note how mysticism and aestheticism tend to merge, this time in a special form of discourse uniquely adapted to the purpose, to provide a special form of insight or rapture.

By thus pushing the aphoristic genre to its uttermost limits Ekelund has, I believe, succeeded in developing a mode of expression uniquely adapted to his aestheticism and, in so doing, integrating thought and form. If such an integration is a criterion of lasting and significant art, Vilhelm Ekelund is indeed a great artist and, I would venture, as an *artist* superior to his philosophical mentor Nietzsche, whose tragic failure, according to Ekelund, was precisely his conspicuous inability to translate his grand vision into art.

This essay began with an attempt to situate Ekelund within the context of Modernism. We noted how the Finnish-Swedish Modernists, the first to "discover" Ekelund's avant-garde prose, regarded him as their mentor and model, stressing his profoundly personal vision and original form. The generation of Swedish Modernist writers in the 1940s in turn "discovered" Ekelund anew, and, given the intellectual climate of the period, stressed his existential and moral commitment.

The question now is how to read Ekelund in the 1980s. The major Swedish writers of today are obviously going elsewhere in search of viable models. Outside Scandinavia, Ekelund is practically unknown, and I know of only one valiant effort to introduce selections from his works to an American audience: Lennart Bruce's excellent *Agenda*.[30] In this essay I have sought to suggest, albeit briefly, new ways to read Ekelund. In so doing I have placed the emphasis on his aesthetic concerns with the nature and function of aphoristic form. I have also sought to explore Ekelund's achievement and significance within a larger comparative context by stressing his affinities with some of the major artist-critics of Modernism, with a tradition characterized by a predisposition for fragmentary forms.

My conclusion is that, from the perspective of the 1980s, Ekelund's aphorisms seem even more radically innovative than they did to the Finnish-Swedish Modernists of the 1920s. His concerns as well as his art do appear decidedly contemporary—post-modern, in fact. The general aspects of Ekelund's works which I have stressed—his aestheticism; his festive approach to ideas; his love of lapidary form; his love of beginnings; his unsystematic philological games, including complex significations, playful etymologies, and the fondness for paradox and allusion; his penchant for mysticism and for Eastern modes of thought; his efforts to transform literary criticism into a form of high art; his absolute commitment to writing as a totally self-contained, free, and gratuitous enterprise; his indifference to history—all these aspects may be found, albeit in a somewhat more radical form, in the later writings of the French critic Roland Barthes, a fact which is less surprising if we recall that Barthes, like Ekelund, owes much to Nietzsche.[31] New developments in literature as well as in criticism do of course change the way we read the writers of the past and thus the course of literary history. From the perspective of the 1980s, and in the wake of a set of radically new ideas about the role and function of criticism, Ekelund appears to have anticipated a number of current trends. But then he always insisted that "forntid är framtid" (antiquity is future).   *Eric O. Johannesson*
University of California

[1] For Lagerkvist's comment on Ekelund, see Nils Gösta Valdén and Algot Werin, eds., *Vilhelm Ekelund: Brev 1917–1949* (Lund: Gleerups, 1970), p. 230.
[2] Olof Enckell, "Under Damoklessvärdet," in *Quosego* (n.p.: n.p., 1928; rpt. Borgå: Söderström, 1971), pp. 27–30.
[3] Susan Sontag, "Reflections. Writing Itself: On Roland Barthes," *The New Yorker*, 26 April 1982, p. 122.
[4] Lars Gyllensten, *Lapptäcken – Livstecken* (Södertälje: Författarförlaget, 1976), p. 220.

[5]K. A. Svensson, *Moralisten-Kulturkritikern* (Stockholm: Fritzes, 1946).

[6]Karl Vennberg, "I lydnad under skönheten," *Kritiskt 40-tal* (Stockholm: Bonniers, 1948), pp. 377–82.

[7]Fredrik Böök, *Resa kring svenska parnassen* (Stockholm: P. A. Norstedt, 1926), pp. 99, 101.

[8]For a remarkable illustration, see Lennart Bruce, "En diktares undergång: Jerry Pena in memoriam," *Horisont*, 30 (1983), 28–41. See also the essay "Medicina mentis: Något om Vilhelm Ekelund och hans läsare," in Carl-Erik af Geijerstam, *Den brutna förtrollningen och andra essayer* (Uddevalla: Författarförlaget, 1979), pp. 63–75.

[9]The expanded version of this interview now available in book form provides important clarifications of Foucault's statement. See Hubert L. Dreyfus and Paul Rabinow, *Michel Foucault: Beyond Structuralism and Hermeneutics*, 2nd ed. (Chicago: University of Chicago Press, 1983), esp. pp. 229–37.

[10]In order to simplify matters, I am using the following set of abbreviations when referring to Ekelund's own works:

A *Attiskt i fågelperspektiv* (Stockholm: Bonniers, 1919)

AH *Atticism-Humanism*, 2nd ed. (Hälsingborg: Tryckeriaktiebolaget Demokraten, 1946)

BL *Båge och lyra 1932* (Stockholm: Bonniers, 1932)

E *Elpidi* (Hälsingborg: Tryckeriaktiebolaget Demokraten, 1939)

L *Lefnadsstämning* (Stockholm: Bonniers, 1925)

M *Metron* (Stockholm: Bonniers, 1918)

PS *Plus salis* (Hälsingborg: Tryckeriaktiebolaget Demokraten, 1945)

VS *Veri similia I–II* (Stockholm: Bonnierbiblioteket, 1963)

[11]The translation of the Greek is "to play well."

[12]Friedrich Nietzsche, *The Gay Science*, trans. Walter Kaufmann (New York: Vintage Books, 1974), no. 366, p. 322.

[13]W. D. Williams, "Nietzsche's Masks," in *Nietzsche: Imagery and Thought*, ed. Malcolm Pasley (Berkeley: University of California Press, 1978), p. 92.

[14]Søren Kierkegaard, *Afsluttende uvidenskabelig efterskrift*, *Samlede Vaerker* (Copenhagen: Gyldendal, 1963), vol. 9, p. 91.

[15]Friedrich Nietzsche, *The Birth of Tragedy*, trans. Francis Golffing (New York: Doubleday, 1956), p. 139.

[16]Hans Meyerhoff, *Time in Literature* (Berkeley: University of California Press, 1955), ch. 2.

[17]Roland Barthes, *Barthes on Barthes* (New York: Hill & Wang, 1977), p. 112.

[18]For a comprehensive analysis of Nietzsche's conception of history, see John Barker, *The Superhistorians: Makers of Our Past* (New York: Scribners, 1982), esp. pp. 209–38.

[19]Algot Werin, *Vilhelm Ekelund 1880–1908* (Lund: Gleerups, 1960), p. 336.

[20]Werin, pp. 357–58.

[21]Werin, p. 390.

[22]Werin, p. 382.

[23]Werin, p. 338.

[24]W. H. Auden and Louis Kronenberger, eds., *The Viking Book of Aphorisms* (New York: Viking, 1963).

[25]Pierre Naert, *Stilen i Vilhelm Ekelunds essayer och aforismer* (Lund: Vilhelm Ekelundsamfundet, 1949).

[26]On *täthet* and other concepts derived from Greek or Latin, see Nils G. Valdén's valuable guide to Ekelund's usage, *Inledning till Vilhelm Ekelund* (Lund: Gleerups, 1965), esp. pp. 64, 125.

[27]Regarding Ekelund's usage of the word "Metron," see Valdén, *Inledning*, pp. 134–35.

[28]The entire aphorism reads as follows: "*On ne peut penser et écrir qu'assis!*" (G. Flaubert). There I have caught you, nihilist! The sedentary life is the very sin against the

Holy Spirit. Only thoughts reached by walking have value." Friedrich Nietzsche, "Twilight of the Idols," in *The Portable Nietzsche*, ed. and trans. Walter Kaufman (New York: Viking, 1954), p. 471.

[29]Robert Linssen, *Living Zen* (London: Allen & Unwin, 1958), p. 44.

[30]Vilhelm Ekelund, *Agenda*, trans. Lennart Bruce (Berkeley: Cloud Marauder Press, 1977).

[31]For a general discussion of Barthes and the tradition of aestheticism, see Sontag, "Reflections." See also the relevant fragments under the following headings in *Barthes on Barthes*: "Aesthetic discourse" (p. 85); "Etymologies" (p. 85); "The circle of fragments" (pp. 92–95); "Beginnings" (p. 94); "Mana-word" (pp. 129–30). Some of the affinities between Barthes and Ekelund have been observed by Per Erik Ljung in his excellent study *Vilhelm Ekelund och den problematisk a författarrollen* (Lund: Liber, 1980). See especially the discussion of Ekelund's erotic feeling for language in *Antikt ideal*, pp. 186–88.

Vilhelm Ekelund's Book Titles Referred to and Abbreviations Used

AG   Agenda (*Agenda*)
AM   Ars Magna (*Ars Magna*)
AH   Atticism–Humanism (*Atticism—Humanism*)
BP   Between Passions (*Passioner emellan*)
BW   Books and Wanderings (*Böcker och vandringar*)
BL   Bow and Lyre (*Båge och lyra*)
CA   Concordia Animi (*Concordia Animi*)
E   Elpidi (*Elpidi*)
EQ   Equinox (*Dagjämningstid*)
FNF   For the Night Falls (*Ty natten kommer*)
ISCL   In Silvis Cum Libro (*In Silvis Cum Libro*)
IUSL   Ius Legendi (*Ius Legendi*)
MW   Menandrean World (*Menandrisk värld*)
M   Metron (*Metron*)
NC   Nordic and Classic (*Nordiskt och Klassiskt*)
OTOS   On the Ocean Shore (*På hafsstranden*)
PS   Plus Salis (*Plus Salis*)
PCLT   Poetry, Criticism, Life and Truth (*Poesi Kritik Sanningsliv*)
NW   The New Watchfulness (*Nya vakten*)
SH   The Salt and Helichrysus (*Saltet och Helichrysus*)
SL   The Second Light (*Det andra ljuset*)
TS   Traces and Signs (*Spår och tecken*)
WE   Western–Eastern (*Väst—Östligt*)
VS   Veri Similia (*Veri Similia*)

EAP   "In Memory of the Centennial of Edgar Poe's Birth"
EJ   Afterword by Eric O. Johannesson
FD   "Flowers of the Destitute"
LB   Introduction and Guide to Key Concepts by Lennart Bruce

Index of Names

Design by David Bullen
Typeset in Mergenthaler Meridien
by Wilsted & Taylor
Printed by Maple-Vail
on acid-free paper